BRINGING GRAPHIC DESIGN IN-HOUSE

ROCKPORT

GLOUCESTER MASSACHUSETTS

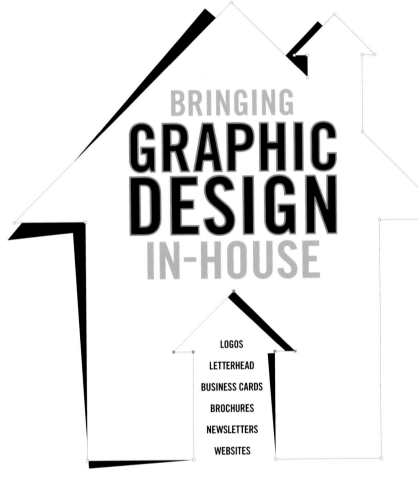

BRINGING

GRAPHIC DESIGN

IN-HOUSE

LOGOS
LETTERHEAD
BUSINESS CARDS
BROCHURES
NEWSLETTERS
WEBSITES

HOW AND WHEN
TO DESIGN IT YOURSELF

ORANGESEED DESIGN

ROCKPORT PUBLISHERS

First published in the United States of America by
Rockport Publishers, Inc.
33 Commercial Street
Gloucester, Massachusetts 01930-5089
Telephone: (978) 282-9590
Fax: (978) 283-2742
www.rockpub.com

Library of Congress Cataloging-in-Publication Data
Bringing graphic design in house : how and when to design it yourself / OrangeSeed Design
    p.   cm.
  ISBN 1-59253-022-2
  1. Commercial art—Technique—Handbooks, manuals, etc. 2. Graphic arts—Technique—Handbooks, manuals, etc. 3. Business communication—Handbooks, manuals, etc.
  I.OrangeSeed design (Firm)
  NC1000.B75 2004
  741.6'068'8—dc22

                                                    2003025958
                                                    CIP

ISBN 1-59253-022-2

10 9 8 7 6 5 4 3 2

Design: OrangeSeed Design

Printed in China

Without the enthusiasm, experience, and dedication of the OrangeSeed Design staff, this book would not have come to be. I would personally like to thank everyone for their contributions to this project and others in our studio that combined to make this book a success.

Phil Hoch, *Art Director*
Rebecca Miles, *Production Designer*
Kristin Lennert Murra, *Account Director*
Dale Mustful, *Design Director*
Jennifer Weisensel, *Graphic Designer*

On behalf of our staff, we would like to acknowledge those who contributed information or insight that played a role in the development of this book, and we extend to them, with sincere gratitude, our heartfelt thanks.

Glenn Arnowitz, *Wyeth and co-founder of InSource*
Andy Epstein, *Gund, Inc. and co-founder of InSource*
Joe Andrews, *West*
Ray Gomez, *Benjamin Moore & Co.*
Lisa Lynch, *Gearworks, Inc.*
David Mataya, *Andersen Corporation*
Ellen Weaver, *Digitas*

In addition, we are grateful to Kristin Ellison, David Martinell, Sarah Chaffee, Kristy Mulkern and everyone at Rockport Publishers for their enthusiasm and support of this project.

Thank You All,
Damien Wolf

CONTENTS

Section One discusses what things you'll need to consider before you decide to bring your design in-house and touches on working relationships with design firms, printers, and other creative resources.

Section Two provides an overview of the major factors of design as it relates to creating effective business communications.

Section Three provides inspiration with actual projects created by in-house designers.

Section Four demonstrates many design styles, which you can use or modify to fit your style, for common design jobs.

Whenever you see this arrow, you will find tips and advice for working with outside design firms, printers, or other creative service providers.

Resources

Information about the resources for type, photography, clip art, and other elements will be provided when appropriate. Details are placed within captions next to related content or in callouts such as this.

Why should a design firm write a book primarily intended to help businesses design things on their own? After all, if we do our job well, this book could potentially take clients away from our studio, as well as others like us.

First, we've been there. Most of our staff has at one time or another worked in an internal creative department. This gives us a unique understanding of the challenges faced by many small businesses, challenges dealing with time, budgets, equipment, software, experience, expertise, personnel—the list is long.

Second, although this book empowers you to design on your own, it also encourages you to look closely at your available resources and to understand when it is in your best interest to work with an outside firm. Knowing when to do it yourself and when to work with outside professionals can be critical to the success of your corporate image and brand development.

Finally, we prefer not to distinguish between "in-house" or "agency" designers. Design is design, whether it's done by someone working at an agency or inside a company. Some of the best design solutions in corporate America come from internal creative departments. Therefore, this book focuses on maximizing your resources to improve your corporate image through design solutions.

This book is written to inform, instruct, demonstrate, and motivate you to develop and maintain the best design solutions that you can. It is written to help non-designers learn more about communications design so that you can feel more comfortable working with outside resources and more confident in your abilities to bring design in-house.

—OrangeSeed Design

BRINGING GRAPHIC DESIGN IN-HOUSE

SECTION ONE:
In-House vs. Hiring It Out

This section walks you through the decision process to help you determine if bringing your design in-house is right for you. Tips for hiring and working with design firms are also provided along with insight into in-house design groups.

DESIGN IT YOURSELF OR HIRE IT OUT?

The boss wants a new logo, your sales team wants new product literature, your website looks like it was made in 1995 (because it was), and you don't even have business cards. Deciding what to do yourself and what to get help with can make a big impact on the success of any business.

One critical factor to successful design is desire. If the person actually doing the work is excited and motivated to design, the results will show it.

Whether you're starting from nothing or building on existing material, creating effective business communication tools can be a challenging task for any size company. To further complicate things, every business situation is unique. Each business has different priorities, different resources, and different goals. However, there is a common link—the need to communicate information about your company and its products or services, to differentiate yourself from your competition. This is where design comes in. Design empowers. It can be the reason someone chooses you over your competitors. It can take two otherwise similar companies and, somehow, make one seem better. For these reasons, and many more, it is important to feel comfortable taking on the challenge and understanding what it takes to be successful. If you do, you'll do great!

We're not trying to scare you off in this section—we know you can do it. But deciding what, when, and how much you can do yourself means asking yourself a few questions. By answering them, you should have a good idea of what you can handle and what you need help with.

Many small businesses assume they can't afford to hire a design firm. Although some firms can be very expensive, many others do excellent work at affordable rates.

QUESTIONS TO ASK YOURSELF:

1. What are my needs?

For most readers, taking on a few design projects will be a lot of work. Therefore, it is important to define what you really need—and we mean *really* need. Sure, it would be great to have that six-color, four-pocket, die-cut, foil-embossed corporate brochure, but do you really need it? Defining your projects by what you need as opposed to what you want will help you keep them to a manageable size.

Focus on your immediate needs and reevaluate from time to time. Once you complete the first few items on your priority list, there are sure to be more!

Now consider your *design* needs. Is image critical to your success? What is the corporate attitude toward design? What are your company's goals, and will design help you get there? These are the questions that determine how important the level of design is to your organization.

2. What resources do I have?

Now you know what you need, so the next question is, do you have (or are you able to get) what you need to get it done?

Start with the basics. Do you have a computer and design or illustration applications to work with? What about printers, fonts, photography, or illustrations? Are there people in the office to help with writing copy or proofreading?

Think about everything you may need, and don't forget about a budget. If you don't handle the finances, someone has to let you know how much you can spend. Even if you design it yourself, you are bound to have incidental costs.

If you're feeling like you're on your own, don't despair. You may have overlooked your biggest resource—you! If you really want to do it yourself, you'll find a way to get what you need. Be creative. Maybe someone in accounting has a digital camera you can use. Or the product development team has a bunch of technical drawings that would look great in a brochure. Whatever it takes, be sure you have (or can get) what you need before you get started.

3. What are my weaknesses?

Be honest with yourself. Are you better at some things than others? Can you take great photographs, but can't draw? Maybe you can write very creative headlines but don't have an interest in long copy. Most people enjoy doing things they are good at, and it shows in their work. If you feel unsure about certain tasks, look for ways to get help in those areas. Most important, being aware of shortcomings will help you overcome them.

4. What are my strengths?

What are you good at? What do you enjoy doing? Do you dream about a new logo at night? Does coming up with a good headline make you giddy? Or, maybe you want to develop your communications strategy and work with someone to create your vision. Whatever it is—focus on it.

To be clear, we're not saying you shouldn't ever take on something new. Sometimes the best way to improve or learn new skills is to accept a new challenge. However, we recommend you first review your *needs* to see if things like the timeframe or quality requirements allow for your learning curve on a new project. Next, review your *resources* to see if you have the means to get training or assistance when you need it.

Make the most of your strengths by leveraging your skills and those of the people around you. By taking a good inventory of the knowledge, ability, and resources you have available, you'll be able to handle much more than you think.

5. What should I do?

At this point, you really only have two choices. Get help, or go for it! You've already decided what you *need*, so there's no sense in delaying your decision. If you're not comfortable taking on a particular project, get help. Otherwise, get started and good luck!

The chart on page 15 details some of the pros and cons of handling your design needs in-house.

Five Steps to Get Started:

1. Define Your Needs

2. Evaluate Your Resources

3. Accept Your Weaknesses

4. Leverage Your Strengths

5. Get Help or *Go for It!*

Resources
Looking for a design firm? There are many places you can start. Try local chapters of the American Institute of Graphic Artists (AIGA; www.aiga.org), or The List (thelistinc.com), the largest online and print database of marketing and advertising professionals.

The Cost of Design

The most common misconception in design is that if you do it yourself you will save money. In some instances this may be true, but in others, it's far from it.

First of all, lets make sure we're talking the same language. Simply put, the cost of design is the sum of all inputs

That extensive list of time-eaters demonstrates that there is a lot more to the cost of design than just design time alone—and we didn't even touch on actual expenses from printers, photographers, and other service providers which you have to factor in as well.

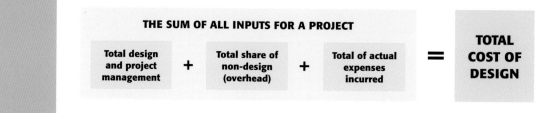

THE SUM OF ALL INPUTS FOR A PROJECT

Total design and project management + Total share of non-design (overhead) + Total of actual expenses incurred = **TOTAL COST OF DESIGN**

that it takes to complete a project. These includes meetings, project management, estimating, concepting time, illustration, copywriting, proofreading, editing, making mockups, working with vendors, attending press checks, and, yes, even the drive time to the printer's shop. But let's not stop there. Don't forget about the half-hour you spent loading a software upgrade, the two hours of work you lost when your file got corrupted, the 17 phone calls and 68 emails you had to respond to, the four hours you spent on the concept design that didn't get used, the hour spent with the boss discussing whether the logo is big enough, or the hour and a half it takes just to clean up your desk and organize all the job information once you're done with a project—*it all counts!*

If you track your time according to each project, like most design firms do, things like loading software and recovering crashed files won't be attributed to a specific job. Instead, these costs are attributed to total overhead costs, which are used to set hourly rates for billable tasks.

The Conveyor-Belt Pulley Theory

Let's assume you make conveyor-belt pulleys for a living. To stay competitive you develop systems and hire good people. You make a quality pulley at a competitive price. You wouldn't expect a design firm to make a pulley for less than a pulley manufacturer could, would you? If not, then don't expect that you can start right out doing graphic design more efficiently than an experienced design firm.

But Can You Save Costs?

Yes, you can save money on design by doing it yourself, but it just doesn't happen on its own. You need to be aware of everything that goes into the process and how to measure your true costs. Often the biggest benefit of in-house design groups is that they keep design costs as internal expenses. This builds assets and adds loyal employees. Over time, these assets become far more valuable than the few dollars you may save on a couple projects.

Design firms often have strong working relationships with illustrators, photographers, printers, and other vendors, which allows them to manage incurred expenses. If you hire out for any of these services, be sure you have clearly outlined estimates of the services you are asking for and that you understand what the vendor will provide before you actually hire them.

PROS AND CONS OF BRINGING DESIGN IN-HOUSE

Cost	**Pro:** You are able to keep many of your expenses as internal costs. **Con:** If you add up all your true costs of labor, overhead, equipment, software, and external vendors that you will still need to work with, it may be difficult to have an overall cost lower than a professional firm that is experienced and efficient at design.
Time	**Pro:** Because all work is done in-house, business owners and marketing staff may feel they receive more attentive response on projects. Opportunities also exist for efficiency in routing projects, meetings, and discussions. **Con:** In addition to actual design time, managing creative projects takes time and expertise. Plan for this while developing schedules and budgets.
Enjoyment	**Pro:** This is one area that is all up to you. If you have a burning desire to do this kind of work every day, then the answer is simple. The creative expression and freedom of design can be exciting and professionally rewarding. **Con:** Design is still a job. If you don't truly enjoy it, the pleasure will fade when things go wrong or as you realize your freedom of expression is now controlled by business decisions.
Control	**Pro:** Keeping design in-house gives you complete control of everything you do. You can easily monitor timelines, budgets, design quality, and more. **Con:** With control comes responsibility. You will have complete ownership of your projects, which is great, until something goes wrong and there's nobody to share the blame.
Quality	**Pro:** Internal designers may feel more ownership of their work as they see a direct impact on the company. Employees are closer to the workflow to monitor the details of each job. **Con:** The quality of work means having quality people doing design, illustration, photography, production, and project management. Finding one person that can do it all is rare, and staffing an entire department increases management and overhead.
Confidentiality	**Pro:** Intellectual property, trade secrets, and other confidential information is much more controllable in an in-house setting. **Con:** There are no general drawbacks, unless you need to keep information from employees, such as mergers, restructurings, or other critical information.
Ownership	**Pro:** Designing it yourself gives you complete ownership of all designs you create (with the exception of any licensing restriction of fonts, illustration, photographs, and so on). **Con:** You need to take time to manage data archival, security, and license enforcement.
Security (Data Safety)	**Pro:** You have access to all of your data at all times. **Con:** Daily backup and long-term archival of data can be expensive and takes time. If it is not part of your normal business systems, you will want to plan for it.
Business	**Pro:** Bringing design in-house may be part of a sound business plan. Issues such as capital purchases, depreciation, expense ratios, and other factors may play a part in why a business may benefit from bringing design in-house. **Con:** Most companies assume they will save money, and this is not necessarily true.

Connect with Other In-House Design Professionals

In-house design departments today face many similar challenges: keeping up with technology advances, staffing, coordinating freelancers, creative work vs. production tasks, job tracking, asset management, charge-backs, inspiring and motivating your staff. To address these issues, Andy Epstein, creative director at Gund, Inc., and Glenn Arnowitz, creative manager at Wyeth, formed InSource, a professional trade organization whose mission is to provide a forum for the advocacy of design excellence in the corporate sector. InSource is committed to providing in-house design directors with the tools necessary to improve productivity, develop expertise, and educate management on the value of design through seminars, training, and dissemination of educational material.

For information about InSource, contact Andy Epstein at aepstein@in-source.org or Glenn Arnowitz at garnowitz@in-source.org, or visit in-source.org

WORKING WITH DESIGN FIRMS

Even companies that handle their own design may still occasionally find themselves in need of a design firm's services. Should this happen to you, knowing how to hire and work effectively with them will not only make your project successful but also cost-effective and enjoyable.

If you're trying to bring design in-house, why would you turn around and hire a design firm? Refer back to the questions on pages 12 and 13 that you asked yourself. Anything you didn't have the resources, experience, or desire to do yourself becomes a perfect example of a project you should hire out.

Consulting

Design firms can act as consultants on anything from picking a company name to setting up an internal graphics department. If you build an on-going relationship with an experienced firm, you'll have someone to turn to whenever you have questions or simply need another professional's opinion. But don't expect them to do it for free. Design is a service business, and time and advice is valuable. If you respect the firm and value their experience, any investment you make in the relationship will pay itself back in the quality of your work and the success of your company.

Overflow

As your company grows, so will your design needs, especially if you do good work. Soon projects will be coming from everyone in your company: marketing, sales, human resources, management, training, and even the person responsible for planning the company picnic. As the work piles up, you may find yourself short on the resources to get it all done. Before you go out and add another designer to your staff, you may consider hiring your overflow work out to an outside resource.

If you just have a small project now and then, you may get by with a free-lance designer. Freelancers are common in graphic design and are extremely flexible. They can often work in your office or take projects home and work on their own equipment.

However, if you continually have too much work you may want to build a relationship with a design firm. You'll benefit from having a team of people that gets to know your needs. They will become familiar with you, your taste, your standards, and the type of projects you bring them. In addition, some firms will offer discounts if they know it is connected to a reliable and on-going flow of work. It never hurts to ask.

People's opinions about design firms often reflect the experiences they've had with them. If you work well with a particular firm, you are more likely to go back to them for a future project.

Working with a design firm is not very different than working with printers, photographers, or other vendors. Sometimes how well you work with the people is as important as the quality of the final work.

Fresh Design

Sometimes an outside perspective on a project can result in an entirely new direction that you wouldn't have taken. Getting a design firm involved can introduce a *fresh look*. You can either have them design the entire project or just hire them to develop a few concept designs—in addition to ones you may create—so you have many options.

Strategies and Systems

Good design firms don't just design. They solve problems. By listening carefully to clients' problems, a firm can draw on the depth of knowledge and related experiences to develop unique solutions to your problems. These solutions often form strategies and systems that guide a company's communications efforts.

Strategies define how you go about doing something. They set rules based on sound business decisions. For instance, brand strategies provide the rationale and direction for building an identity around a product or company. They can also guide the relationship between related brands, such as between parent and subsidiary companies. Communication strategies define approaches for the messages and mediums you'll use to convey a message to an audience. Strategies can be complex or very basic and can be used to define solutions for just about any problem.

Systems provide structure for how various elements work together to achieve a specific result. On a broad level, a *design system* is made up of the elements that make all of your design projects look like they are part of the same family. On a smaller scale, a *collateral system* may contain a folder, brochures, flyers, and other information that all work together.

The specific result is to have a communications kit that is customizable for each potential customer.

In addition to design, systems can include processes, such as this simple example for a sales process:

1. Send out direct mail.
2. Follow up with a phone call.
3. Send out a customized collateral system.
4. Schedule an appointment.
5. Follow up with a corporate thank-you card.
6. Create a proposal.
7. Close the sale.

Notice how this process included potential design elements—direct mail, a collateral system, a corporate thank-you card, and a proposal—all of which are part of a system designed to close a sale.

Working with a design firm can often help you define strategies and put systems in place that provide direction and structure for your future internal communication design needs.

Special Needs

Some projects will inevitably require a skill set that neither you nor anyone around you has. It may be a lack of experience, or it may come from a lack of equipment. Either way, you may end up going outside for help.

Some examples of this may include: writing technical manuals, editing extremely large images, designing three-dimensional packaging, programming a website, creating die-lines for complex projects, integrating email marketing, conducting focus groups or other types of research, and many more. It could be anything—and a special need for one company may not be difficult at all for another. Every situation is unique.

Projects Companies Hire Out:

Companies hire out the type of projects that are not a good fit for their internal staff. This list is not comprehensive.

Overflow work

Long projects with extensive production, like catalogs or manuals

High-level production work, such as image editing and color corrections

Illustration and photography

Package design

Strategic branding and communications initiatives

Corporate or product identity systems

Technical documentation

Research and focus groups

Regularly published editorial documents like newsletters or magazine inserts

Hiring a Design Firm

There is an abundance of selection when it comes to graphic design firms. It is important to remember that the quality of work you receive doesn't depend upon the size or location of the studio, or whether they've been featured in national design magazines. What matters is that they provide a high-quality, professional service that meets your needs and that you work well together.

Conduct Your Search

Finding a design firm often starts by asking people you know for referrals. Other business owners and marketing executives, printers, photographers, and design instructors at local universities can all be excellent sources of information. In addition, business directories or trade organizations can also provide leads. The American Institute of Graphic Arts is a non-profit organization with local chapters scattered across the country. Their website (aiga.org) provides resources that can help link you to members of your local design community.

Narrow the Candidates

Depending on the size of your community, you may find 20 or more reputable firms. In larger cities there will be literally hundreds of options if you include qualified freelancers. Most professional firms will have a website that shows some samples of their work, describes their philosophy, and provides basic information about their studio and the services they offer. Call any that interest you to discuss your project and their experience to see if there is a good fit. Select no more than five for a personal interview.

Interview Firms

If you can, meet at the design firm's studio. Seeing where and how they work can often tell you a lot about their work style. It also gives you a chance to meet some of their staff. Ask to see samples of work, especially things that are similar to your project. Be prepared to provide as much information about your needs as you can. The firm will want to know about your company, your market, and the project details to be able to fully understand your needs. Pay attention to how a firm proposes they will go about solving your unique problem, as much as you do the samples you review.

Understand Business Practices

Before you choose a firm, make sure you understand how the business relationship will work. Ask about things like billing rates, estimates, how changes are handled, who pays expenses, or how you are invoiced. Lastly, be sure both you and the design firm understand what services will be provided and what they will cost. Having these details outlined in writing beforehand will help eliminate confusion later on.

Make Your Selection

Graphic design is a service business that is built around the personal relationships between agency and client, as much as it is around the actual work being performed. You will spend a lot of time interacting with the firm, so be sure you feel comfortable working with them. If you like the people, the processes, the work, and the price, you've likely found your firm.

Questions to Ask When Hiring a Design Firm:

What types of client do you work with? Can you tell me about them?

What type of work have you done that is similar to this project?

What are your processes?

How do you bill clients?

Who in your firm will actually be working on my projects? Who will be our main contact?

What experience do you have that relates to my industry or my business?

What are some of your firm's biggest accomplishments?

What are the long-term plans for your firm?

Do you have a back-up system?

Your Role as a Client

Once you've hired a design firm, your job doesn't stop here. To be successful you will need to be involved throughout the entire project. How much will depend on the size of the job and your management style, as well as the design studio's processes. But even if there is someone at the firm responsible for managing the project, you are ultimately in control. It is your role to provide leadership and direction to everyone involved.

Set Your Expectations

Foremost, set your expectations in the form of goals for your project and clearly communicate them. This will help provide direction and a way to measure results upon completion. Anything you wish to accomplish should be stated up front, or it may not happen.

Also, set your own expectations. For instance, if you are asking your designers to work on a very small budget, don't be upset when the design is fairly simple. Good design is not always fast, and it isn't usually cheap. Designers will balance the creative solutions they develop and the production costs to stay within your budget, so if you don't give them much, don't expect much.

Provide Direction

Your role is to provide your firm with direction for the project, which usually comes in the form of a creative brief. Some people may call them creative blueprints, project initiation forms, or other names, but their purpose is all the same.

Creative briefs clearly outline the audience, objectives, positioning, key copy points, budgets, schedule, requirements, restrictions, and any other information that the design team will need to know. A thorough creative brief not only will provide direction but act as a reference point for judging creative solutions and evaluating your final results.

The creative brief is usually put together by the client; however, many design firms will work with you to write one if you are unfamiliar with them.

Reviews, Feedback, and Approval

Another role you will have is to provide timely review of all design concepts and layouts. This includes routing everything to internal co-workers who need to review the project. You should then review all comments and summarize the changes you would like the design firm to make. Doing this in a timely manner is critical to keeping your project on schedule. Lastly, you will be responsible for final approval before production begins.

Build Relationships

Often, after projects are completed there is a feeling of relief and a break to relax. But before you file everything away and jump into the next project, take time to review the end results against your goals. Evaluate the process and interaction with your design firm and provide feedback to them. A simple thank-you or word of appreciation will go a long way when your next project comes up.

Should You Tell Them What Your Budget Is?

Clients often feel that they shouldn't tell what their budget is because the design firm will just go ahead and spend all the money, when a cheaper solution could have worked.

This isn't always true. If you have $50,000 you can spend, but you would really like to spend only $40,000 so you can do another project with the balance, then tell them so. This sets parameters for the firm to follow. Without budget guidelines, the creative solution could come back over $50,000 just as easily.

It really comes back to building a good working relationship with a firm that you trust.

BRINGING IT IN-HOUSE!

If you've decided to bring your graphic design in-house, congratulations, and welcome to the exciting and challenging field of design. Now that you are a designer, there is no reason the work you do can't be just as good—if not better—than that coming from a design firm.

Internal design groups must constantly balance the creative and business needs of their company. Designers must have the ability to clearly communicate with their fellow designers and with the various levels of management.

However, there may be some differences in the resources you have, the office environment in which you're working, or a number of other things you'll encounter working in a corporate setting that are different than in a creative studio. This is not to say you can't try to emulate the creative setting and resources often associated with design firms. But then, do you really need to? Every company is unique, and the design that comes out of it should be as well. Be yourself and create an environment that you and the rest of your company are comfortable working in. Let's look at some of the opportunities and challenges you'll come across.

Project Variety

Just imagine all the things you can do! Whether it's new media presentations for sales meetings, websites, packaging, catalogs, or collateral, there are many ways to get your company's message across. There are also multiple audiences your company has to reach! The range of opportunity is exciting and will keep you and other designers interested and engaged.

Establish a relationship with two or three printers, photographers, copywriters, sign companies, display manufacturers, or other vendors you may need to work with by touring their businesses and getting to know the people you will work with.

Future Plans

Think of the big picture: where do you want your company to be five or ten years from now? How will bringing design in-house help you get there? Make design part of your business plan, and aspire to be better then than you are now, keeping your company's best interests in mind, too. Take chances. Go out on a limb for design you believe in, and take on projects that you may be nervous about. Without doing so, your skills won't stretch and grow.

Designer or Department

Are you a solo designer in a smaller company or are you building an entire in-house department? Design needs may not vary between the two, but equipment and management needs will be far more extensive with a department.

Many of the following in-house design considerations are written as if you are building a department, but they address issues that apply to solo or small-office designers as well.

In-House Design Considerations

Getting Started

Many designers are simply given a directive to "start an in-house design department." Easier said than done, right? Here are some guidelines to help you out and ideas to keep management firmly on your side.

Call or meet the managers of established in-house graphics departments from other corporations to observe how their departments are structured. What can you learn from their successes and failures? Out of these discussions, create a guide and timeline for your own department.

Get to know the phrase "return on investment." The people you report to will want to know what the payback will be and how long it will take. You'll be asked to justify every expenditure, no matter if it's an equipment purchase, additional staff, or even printing costs. Make a good, sensible business argument for the things you're requesting.

Spend time developing relationships with upper management and "lower" management. You'll have to delegate to subordinates as well report to superiors. Cultivate interaction with various department heads, even in areas that might not seem, on the surface, to need design services. As you become comfortable with these colleagues, it will be easier for you to really understand what their needs are, as well as make them see where you're coming from.

Establishing an Identity

Many in-house departments suffer from an identity crisis. Unlike advertising agencies or design firms whose livelihood depends on how they communicate to prospective clients, in-house departments' clients are internal and projects will come from anywhere: the marketing department, the trade show division, the new product launch team. But sometimes these groups don't really know what the in-house team is truly capable of.

Other internal designers struggle as they become less creative and more production-oriented. Sometimes that's how an in-house department starts, by accident or on a per-project, as-needed basis. Technology has made it easier and more affordable to handle production functions, but the time spent on those activities is time taken away from being creative.

How do you combat these challenges? Make your department the expert in design—visual identity—for your entire organization. Become indispensable to every business group in the company, and try to meet their needs, whether it's printed material, signage, uniforms, or anything else that needs designing. And if you can't provide something, find out who can and be a liaison between that source and your internal client.

Do things to market your department within the company. Some in-house departments have achieved bigger and more important projects through a strong internal advertising campaign. Create a website showcasing your work. Distribute flyers touting your efficiency and cost-consciousness. Submit articles to the company newsletter about a recent project or a new service. Anything and everything you can do to get the word out will change (and improve!) the image of your department and how it is perceived by those who will need your services.

My staff consists of a group of seasoned professionals with traditional design skills who are very passionate about their work. They have a strong commitment to high standards and client satisfaction and can easily shift priorities, depending upon business needs. Strong personal initiative is a trait I look for when hiring full-time or freelance designers and the ability to follow through on projects from concept to print (not to mention the ability to use an x-acto knife).

Glenn John Arnowitz
Manager, Corporate Graphics
Wyeth

Managing In-House Design

Many in-house design or creative managers are also designers, people who have come up through the ranks and take on projects themselves as well as oversee an entire department. But as the department manager, you need business acumen, too. You have to think as a designer and a business person, while balancing creative needs, timelines, budgets, personnel issues, and other tasks.

If you've never managed people before, it can be intimidating. Even if only two or three designers work in the department, keeping things on track is critical. Consider holding project review meetings to discuss both current and upcoming work. Create processes and forms to traffic projects as they move through your system. Rotate projects so no one is saddled for too long with a single project. Consider bringing in freelancers if the staff is buried.

In-house designers are not always viewed as "artists." They are well-rounded individuals with important assets: a broad knowledge of the company's product or service, good communication skills with colleagues, organizational and management abilities to handle project logistics, and a strong understanding of production and printing procedures. Not all in-house design departments are large enough to have an account manager, a traffic coordinator, or an administrative assistant on staff to handle non-design work. In-house designers are valued not only for their strong design skills but also for their all-around abilities.

Whereas these aren't skills inherent in everyone, many companies encourage their staff to attend personal development activities to improve these and other abilities. When it comes to training, a knee-jerk reaction for designers is always to take a computer course. But management and communication skills can be just as valuable.

Hiring Diverse Designers

It is important to assemble a good team of people who are willing to interact, share ideas, and grow together as designers. All designers are not equal. One person might not be able to conceptualize but may have great experience with production, and another person might be a better illustrator but not a very good communicator. A good manager can turn these diversities into assets and use each designer's expertise to the benefit of the department, simultaneously challenging each designer to grow.

Hire designers with complementary skills. Make sure your group has the right combination of design, production, and management skills for your company's needs. Different designers might have varied experiences with anything from photography, printing and production techniques, paper familiarity, and copywriting to computer networking and troubleshooting and Internet programming. Diverse designers will help build a more well-rounded internal team.

Motivating Designers

An ongoing challenge is keeping designers motivated and stimulated so they continue to produce innovative work. Empower individual designers by providing them with entire projects to oversee. Encourage a variety of inspiring exercises to keep the creative juices flowing—things like occasional "show and tell" sessions to share ideas, articles, books, and design trends. Acknowledge outstanding

Do what designers do! If you want to establish a creative environment, attend design group events, tour printers, read industry publications, and constantly push the creative envelope.

achievements when the group is together. Plan fun and casual group events like bowling or picnics that encourage social interaction.

Tracking Time

Whether you have one designer or twenty, everyone should record the amount of time he or she spends on each project. Various software applications make this very simple, but a simple spreadsheet works fine, too. By tracking your time to a specific job, department, or task, you will begin to see how long different types of jobs take for future planning purposes, you can bill back your internal costs to another department's budget, and, most important, you can justify the value of your work to the company. This last reason will back you up with a bit of job security should your company ever begin looking for ways to cut expenses.

Leveraging Technology

Technology moves fast. As an internal group you may be responsible for your own equipment and technology systems. Do your research and choose proven technology over unproven promises. If your systems need to work with other departments, make sure they are able to. Evaluate your equipment, software, training, and support on a regular basis, and be prepared to justify all purchases to your business owner or finance department.

Working with Design Firms

There's no getting around it: sometimes an outside creative resource is necessary. Earlier in this section we discussed a number of reasons an internal design group would hire an outside design resource, of which there are many.

What we didn't discuss was how you can still provide a service to your internal customers by managing their projects and having the work done by an outside source. It is an excellent service you can offer to them, because many people won't be comfortable doing it themselves. In addition, this gives you the opportunity to control the creative development so that any branding initiatives or style guidelines you've been working to establish are still followed.

The risk you run by telling your internal clients "We can't do this" is that they may find someone outside that handles not only this project for them but also all their other projects. Unless your company mandates that everyone bring all work through the internal design group, you run the risk of losing work, which hurts your job security. Simply establishing a relationship with an outside source for overflow work will eliminate this problem. You never know, you may even find that teaming up with an outside graphic design source can be rewarding, enjoyable, and educational for everyone involved.

It's really exciting to be an in-house designer, in part due to the range of design opportunities presented. It's not only the types of project but also the various audiences our company has to reach. We create teddy bears that are sold for $1,000 each as well as the $5 impulse buy: There's a totally different kind of graphic feel, message, and audience for both. We get to be high-end and elegant as well as cartoony and fun. It keeps the whole group interested and engaged!

Aaron Epstein
Creative Director
Gund, Inc.

BRINGING GRAPHIC DESIGN IN-HOUSE

SECTION TWO:
In-House Design Basics

This section discusses design basics, starting with a defini-
tion as it pertains to this book. General aspects of business
communication as well as individual design elements are
both described and demonstrated with a variety of examples.

WHAT IS DESIGN?

Design covers many things, but for the purpose of this book, we're referring to everything involved in the creation of business communications. This not only means preparing an actual layout but also includes the project management, copywriting, proofreading, budgeting, and production involved in completing a finished project, whether it is in print or an interactive medium.

Design can be and do many things. It is a tool that, when used properly, can contribute greatly to a company's success but, if used poorly, can have the same degree of negative impact.

Why define design so broadly? Mostly because if you are planning on bringing design in-house, you are actually bringing in a whole lot more than simply the actual design stage. And this applies to everyone from a solo designer to entire internal creative departments.

We've also focused on business communications design because that's what most companies need. Corporate communications design is much different than design as a fine art. Your goal is to create material that contributes to the success of your company. It's not just about making cool business cards or getting to do a fancy die-cut brochure, unless those things benefit your company. And while you should always be passionate about your work, don't be so attached that you become frustrated when management demands you change it. Push the envelope, but be prepared to justify your designs with solid business reasons.

Design Is Problem Solving

Every design challenge has multiple solutions. What makes one better than another is how well it solves the problem at hand. Does a brochure need to be bright and colorful to stand apart from others, or would making it very big and having a special die-cut make it stand out more? Could a square soup can sell better than a round one? Is it more affordable to design and distribute three small product brochures or one large brochure covering all three products? These are simple examples of problems design must solve. In addition, there are many communication challenges designers must address to effectively get the desired message to the right audience. How design communicates is discussed further on page 27.

Design Is a Process

To solve problems, design must follow a process. Good design doesn't just happen. It inherently follows basic steps, which will be outlined later in the Design Process section. These steps include having a thorough understanding of the design challenge, developing and evaluating solutions, and working to completion. No matter how brief each step is, they exist in nearly all design projects.

Design as a communication tool can be used in many ways. By combining various elements of design such as color, type, and images, the ways to convey a message are limitless.

Communicate Personality

Have you ever seen a person show strong feelings toward a particular product or company? Take Apple Computer, for example. Millions of people literally get excited just talking about Apple's products. They have a cult-like following of loyal customers that is rivaled only by the likes of Harley-Davidson or possibly Coca-Cola. Why do some people love Apple? Because Apple presents an image of style and innovation in everything they do, which communicates personality traits that millions of people want to associate with. Apple spends millions of dollars in design each year to make sure people don't just buy computers, they buy *cool* computers.

Communicate Messages

Design communicates messages through any combination of words, images, or graphics. An appropriate image can often say as much or more than words can, and a combination of the two can be even stronger. Be cautious that the images you select enhance the message you are sending. Images can be interpreted differently by different people, so it is important that your text and images don't conflict or cause confusion for the viewer.

Graphic elements such as lines, arrows, and boxes are often used to draw attention to, isolate, or group information so the message is easier for people to process.

Communicate Emotion

Similar to communicating personality, but much more personal, is emotion. Design works best when it not only communicates an emotion but actually creates an emotion in the viewer. For example, if you see an ad with a sad child, you understand the emotion of the child. However, if the combination of the image and the words that go with it are strong enough to actually make you feel sad, then that is powerful design.

Think about some of the ads you see on a regular basis: phone companies trying to remind you of someone you miss so you'll call them (loneliness), coffee makers trying to convince you to share a cup with someone you love (romance), or beauty products that promise to reduce the effects of aging (fear). Why do advertisers do this? Because they know that for many people, purchasing decisions are made on an emotional level. This is not to say that the advertisers are doing something bad. Relating to someone's emotions is the easiest way to clearly communicate what a product is all about. As long as it is truthful, it is a smart way to design.

The Good and the Bad

If there is one truth about design, it is that it always communicates something. Good or bad, people will get some sort of impression from each encounter they have with your company. And each exposure to everything from your business cards, letterhead, and envelopes to your website, packaging, and invoices is an opportunity to present a positive message about your products and your company.

This promotion conveys the message of family fun. Use your hand to cover up the photograph at the bottom, and see how much emotion is lost.

WHAT YOU'LL NEED

Handling all of your graphic design needs can be a big responsibility that requires planning and preparation. If you are a small company, this may be a simple step, but if you are a larger company that is planning to build an internal design department, you'll need to approach things from a whole different level. Either way, your basic considerations will be very similar.

Being well-outfitted can contribute to the enthusiasm and creativity of your internal design group. Although having the right tools won't make you a good designer, they will make a good designer more efficient.

It will make your job much easier if you are on the same computer platform as the printers, design firms, or other vendors you work with. If you can, ask these vendors what system they prefer.

This section outlines the basic equipment, software, and even general office items you will need to be well equipped to take on any design project. But before we get into the details, let's talk a bit about what you'll need to get everything you need.

How to Get It

If your reason for bringing design in-house has anything to do with saving money, then the first challenge you're going to face is justifying the purchases you'll need just to get started. You may already have some of the basics, such as a computer and general office equipment, but you'll need to make sure all the new things you buy will work with your existing equipment before you buy anything.

Unless you are the person in charge of purchasing, you are going to need to prepare an estimate of all the equipment and software you wish to purchase. Take time to investigate all your choices, and plan out what are essential items and what can be cut in case you don't get approval to buy everything at one time.

If you have management's backing to bring this work in-house, then they should also be willing to support you with the proper equipment to allow you to do your job effectively. If they are not supportive, try to get them to see the long-term benefits of their investment. Without the proper tools, you will not be able to perform efficiently, and it will be more difficult to work with printers and other vendors. If this is the case, you might be better off sticking with outside resources who are set up for this type of work.

Mac or PC: What's Right for You

The majority of the design community uses Macintosh computers. The majority of the business community uses Windows PCs. So which do you use? Unfortunately, it isn't an easy answer. You'll have to evaluate your internal systems, including existing equipment, software, and network infrastructure. The most popular design and publishing software applications are cross-platform, as are most of the popular word processing and general office programs, so your decision may come down to personal preference.

This decision is, however, a very important one, because it will have a large impact on all future purchases of both hardware and software. It also will be important if you plan to work with outside printers, design firms, or other service providers. It helps if you are on the same platform as these vendors because, although a software program may run on both Mac and PC, the layout files you create may not transfer 100 percent correctly unless all fonts and images are also available on the other system.

Whereas some design firms actually use Macs for all design and production work, they use a few PCs for business and accounting functions. If you are starting from scratch, you can just as easily buy all the same platform, but integrating new machines with existing ones is a good way to make use of any assets your company has. Any money you save will help justify bringing your design in-house.

Graphic Design Equipment Checklist

Basic equipment and supply needs can be grouped into three main categories: hardware, software, and general office equipment and supplies. Within each are many selections from which to choose.

Macintosh G5, Apple Computer, www.apple.com

Hardware
☐ Computer (Mac or PC)
☐ Monitor
☐ Printer
☐ Scanner
☐ Digital Camera
☐ Backup System
☐ File and Print Server
☐ Gadgets

Software
☐ Page Layout
☐ Illustration
☐ Image Editing
☐ Font Management
☐ PDF Creation and Management
☐ Time Tracking and Project Management
☐ Prepress and Preflight
☐ General Office
☐ Fonts

General Equipment and Supplies
☐ General Office Equipment
☐ Flat Files and Secured Storage
☐ PANTONE Color Matching Books
☐ Paper Stock and Paper Samples
☐ Cutting Boards, Rulers, and Knives
☐ Light Table
☐ Spray Booth
☐ Fine Art Supplies
☐ Mounting and Display Boards

Resources
For more on whether Macs or PCs are right for you, check out graphicsiq.com. The site is dedicated to helping designers and creative professionals with real-world, practical information on new products, best practices, news, tips, and techniques.

For designers using Mac systems, the G5 is currently the top of the line. It offers dual processors and plenty of memory and storage configuration options to work effectively for just about anyone.

Graphic design firms typically archive jobs for later retrieval, but not all printers and service bureaus do. It is best to have your own archival system so you don't have to rely on others to retrieve your files if you need them in the future.

Hardware

For each type of hardware you need there are many different brands, models, and features. Talking to other people in the industry and reading product reviews will help you decide which to choose.

Computers

As mentioned earlier, the debate over using Macintosh or Windows PCs is a big one. It will probably be the biggest decision you'll make in setting up your system, because it will affect all of your other hardware and software purchases, now and in the future.

Many of the arguments for using one platform over the other do not mean as much today as they once did, because for the most part, both systems can do the same things. Major layout and design programs are available for both systems. Common word processing, spreadsheet, and presentation files can be transferred seamlessly between platforms. Macs and PCs can easily share files on the same network. And the speed of each computer varies greatly based on its processor, the amount of memory you have, the speed of your hard drive, and the applications you are running. So, it is not as much about which platform you choose, as it is about how you configure the computer you choose.

With that said, Macs have historically dominated the graphic design industry, both in studios and with other vendors with whom you'll likely collaborate. Take the time to see what the people you will be working with recommend and compare that with your internal abilities to support either platform.

Once you have made your decision, it is time to configure your system so that you can effectively do graphic

design. Typically, design systems will need to be better equipped than than a general office computer because the files you work with are much larger and the software used performs functions that are much more complex.

Processor: The speed of the processor affects the number of calculations your computer can perform each second. The faster the processor, the more calculations. Word processing requires much less power than image editing, which in turn requires much less than video editing.

Memory: Memory greatly affects your overall system performance, because the more you have, the less your computer will access data from hard drives, which are much slower. You can never have too much.

Storage: Your primary means of file storage will be on hard drives. Because graphic files can easily be tens and sometimes hundreds of megabytes, it is important to have plenty of storage. You can either store files on a hard drive in your computer, on an external drive connected to your computer, or on a network file server.

In addition to these major factors, you may consider adding CD- or DVD-writing capabilities for file transferring, network or wireless communications, and anything else you think you will be necessary to do your job effectively.

Monitors

Monitors typically last more than five years, whereas your computer may be outdated in less than three. Because of this, it makes sense to get a large, high-quality monitor that will allow you to work efficiently on large layouts without scrolling back and forth all the time. Monitors range from 15" to 23" (380mm to 580mm). Get the biggest one you can— you won't regret it.

Most designers are moving away from older CRT (cathode ray tube) monitors and towards LCD (liquid crystal display) displays. Although LCDs are often more expensive than CRT monitors, they offer flat screens that take up less space, are brighter, flicker less, and use less power. Plus, they look cool!

Printers

If you plan on designing more than just a few projects a year, invest in a color laser printer. If possible, get one that will print on a variety of paper sizes, up to 12" x 18"(300mm x 460mm) or larger. You'll appreciate being able to proof full tabloid-size pages without have to tile multiple pages together.

Scanners

Modern scanners provide very good quality even in your entry- to mid-range models. Look for features such as slide or transparency capabilities if you will need to scan anything besides reflective art. A basic model should deliver results suitable for many online projects. If you plan to do a lot of high-end scanning, send the work out to a service bureau.

Digital Cameras

With the price of digital cameras dropping and their quality getting better and better, they have become commonplace for most designers. They make it simple to quickly get concept or production-ready images into your designs. If you plan to use the images you shoot for final production, be sure you get a camera that has enough resolution. In the digital world, that means a minimum of five megapixels.

Backup System

Backing up your files is a must. You never know when a hard drive or a file will become corrupted. Believe it—it will happen eventually. A backup system can be as simple as copying critical files to another hard drive, a CD, or other storage device. If you have a lot of files or many computers, look into a tape backup system with automated backup software.

File and Print Server

If you have many people working on related files, you'll find a central file server will make your life much easier. If your company has a server in place, be sure you are allocated enough storage space for your files. A print server allows multiple people to print to the same printer at one time by putting all print jobs in a queue and processing from the server.

Gadgets

There are plenty of gadgets to get excited about, but make sure you have your basic needs taken care first—then do your fun shopping.

Backing Up vs. Archiving

A backup system duplicates incremental changes to important files on a regular basis–daily or weekly, depending on your needs. Archiving is done at the end of a project. It entails cleaning up all files and selecting the important ones you may need in the future. Then you should make one or more copies on CDs, DVDs, or digital tapes. Duplicate copies are preferred in case one is lost or damaged.

Resources

In addition to local retailers and buying direct from manufacturers, you can find most of the hardware and software you need from online resellers like MacWarehouse (macwarehouse.com) and MicroWarehouse (microwarehouse.com), or MacZone (maczone.com) and PCZone (pczone.com).

Most of today's design and layout applications are available for both Mac and PC computers. These are Extensis Suitcase, Adobe Illustrator, and Adobe Photoshop icons as they appear in the Mac OS X dock.

Make sure any freelancers, design firms, or vendors have the same version of fonts that you use. Like other software applications, you should not provide your fonts to others to use on their systems. Check your font licenses for specific usage rights and restrictions.

Software

Some applications claim to do it all—layout, illustration, and image editing. However, most professional designers use different programs for each function, along with a host of supporting programs.

Page Layout

Professional page layout software must provide extensive tools for building complex and varied documents, arranging graphics, and controlling type.

Three programs lead this category. Quark Xpress has been the dominant player for more than a decade. Adobe InDesign is a relative newcomer to the field but has received a lot of attention and is gaining popularity. InDesign integrates well with Adobe's illustration and image editing programs, which we will discuss later. Adobe Pagemaker, which was the industry leader in the early days of desktop publishing, has declined in popularity. With new versions of Quark Xpress and InDesign bringing new and innovative features to designers' toolset, the choice is a tough one.

Ask for advice from designers in your area, and talk with vendors you may need to share files with. They may prefer one format over the other.

Illustration

Illustration programs produce vector artwork, which can be scaled to any size without losing quality. For logos and other artwork, vector graphics are the preferred format with designers and commercial printers. Although advanced illustration programs do provide very good page-layout tools, they are used more commonly for special projects like package design or printed pieces with special die-cuts. They do not typically provide support needed for multiple-page, complex documents. Adobe Illustrator, CorelDraw, and Deneba Canvas are all available in Mac and PC versions.

Image Editing

Image-editing programs provide pixel-based manipulation of photographs and other bitmap images. These programs should allow you to open and export a wide variety of graphic formats for print and web use. Common file formats include EPS, JPG, GIF, and TIFF files, as well as many more for specialized needs.

Adobe Photoshop and Corel Photo-Paint have set the benchmarks for this category of software. The programs offer tools for enhancing color, contrast, and saturation, as well tools for special effects like blurring, sharpening, and texturizing images. Photo layering and compositing features also enable advanced manipulation of your artwork.

Font Management

As a designer, you will likely use many fonts. Finding, organizing, and activating them can be cumbersome. You can't keep them all turned on at once or you will take up too much memory and slow down your computer.

Font management software allows you to group type by project, style, client, or any other way you wish. It allows you to quickly preview them to find what you're looking for. Plus, it will activate fonts automatically when you open a file that uses a font that is not in use.

Popular options include software from Extensis, Apple, and Adobe.

PDF Creation and Management

Portable Document Format (PDF) files have become the standard way to share documents with people on any platform without needing the application in which the file was originally created. In addition you can create PDF forms that can be filled out on a computer instead of on paper. And for advanced users, you can review documents and make comments that will be saved in the file. At a minimum you will need the Adobe Acrobat Reader, which is free and allows you to open PDF files. If you plan to share documents with non-designers, you'll want to look into the rest of the Acrobat family of products.

Time Tracking and Project Management

Time tracking is a necessity in the design business and is a good idea for internal designers, too—even if you're not required to do so. Some inexpensive programs specialize in just time recording and reporting, whereas complex studio management solutions help you manage entire jobs, including time, expenses, schedules, and invoicing. Depending on your needs, consider Clients & Profits or DesignSoft's Time and Billing.

Prepress and Preflight

Interrupting the production process due to poorly prepared files is one of the most common, and often costly, mistakes designers make—which is unfortunate because there are easy and affordable software solutions that collect all necessary fonts and images, report suspected problems, and automatically compress files for delivery to your printer.

If you plan to have your projects professionally printed, applications like Extensis Collect Pro (for Macs) or Markzware's Flightcheck (for Macs and PCs) are definitely worth purchasing.

General Office

Even as a designer you are likely to have a need for basic word processing, spreadsheet, presentation, and database applications. It may be simply to exchange brochure text with a copywriter or to keep a table of project-related expenses, but you will no doubt need at least a few of them from time to time. You will almost definitely need an email program and web browser.

Not so ironically, the leaders in all these categories also create your two main operating systems: Apple and Microsoft. At the bottom of this page is a chart listing the applications both companies develop and the platforms they run on.

fonTS

Fonts are a form of software with rules about their use, similar to the applications you purchase. Like other programs, when you purchase a font you are actually purchasing a license to use it. How you can use it is described in the license agreement that comes with it.

Fonts can be purchased individually or in packages containing anywhere from just a few to thousands.

For a basic identity system, most companies decide on two or three different fonts. This is highly recommended for building consistency in all of your design projects. However, when the need arises for a creative typeface, there are a myriad to choose from.

Category	Microsoft	Apple
Word Processing	Word (Mac/PC)	Works (Mac*)
Spreadsheet	Excel (Mac/PC)	Works (Mac*)
Presentation	PowerPoint (Mac/PC)	Keynote (Mac*)
Email	Outlook (PC) Entourage (Mac)	Mail (Mac*)
Database	Access (PC)	FileMaker Pro (Mac/PC)
Browser	Explorer (Mac/PC)	Safari (Mac)

*These applications are compatible with the corresponding Microsoft product.

It may seem primitive to have supplies like adhesives and boards on hand in today's digital world, but there will be more need for these products than you think.

It is very important to provide full-size mockups of your projects to your production vendor to avoid mistakes and avoid confusion about size, folds, or other details that can't be easily seen in the file.

General Equipment and Supplies

Just like other departments, you'll use your share of pencils and paper clips, but you'll also have some things that others may not. Keep the ones you use most in stock so they're there when you need them.

General Office Equipment

Other than your color laser printer, which you'll want to reserve for design use, you should be able to share the general office fax, copier, printer, and other equipment. There's no use in buying it twice if you don't need it.

Flat Files and Secured Storage

Flat files are very handy for storing paper samples, press sheets you've pulled and want to save, and any other large-format material you have. Plus, have some form of lockable storage where you can keep software, cameras, and other equipment that you don't want to have borrowed and lost.

PANTONE Color Matching Books

If you're producing print work, at least one set of PANTONE Color Matching Books are a necessity. Ideally you'll have a coated, uncoated, and process conversion guide.

Paper Stock and Samples

You never know when you'll need to mock up a large brochure or assemble a large folder to demonstrate a design concept. Having a variety of paper types, weights, and sizes will come in handy. Also keep paper swatchbooks of various paper samples on hand. You can get them free from any major paper supplier.

Cutting Boards, Rulers, and Knives

A soft, self-healing cutting board, metal-edged rulers, and X-ACTO knives are essential to assembling clean mockups of brochures and other projects. Keep plenty of sharp blades on hand, and be sure to get a few rulers in different lengths. It makes it easier to work on very small or very large layouts if you have a ruler that is close in size.

Light Tables

A light table is great to have when you are reviewing photo transparencies, although with digital photography this occurs less and less often. However, if you have one, you'll be surprised at how often you use it to trace artwork or align registration marks on mockups.

Spray Booth and Supplies

Not only will having a proper spray booth make it easier for you to make mockups, it will keep your office free from sticky adhesives and keep potentially harmful vapors out of the air.

Fine Art Supplies

If you or anyone in your office plans to use traditional mediums, you may need acrylic or oil paint, brushes, canvas, drawing paper, pastels, or any number of fine art materials.

Mounting and Display Boards

Keep both black and white foam board and/or matte board in your office so you can mount your designs for presentation to management or for display in your work area to showcase your work to other employees.

DESIGN DEPARTMENT SUPPLY ORDER FORM

Supplier Phone: 888-555-1000 Fax: 888-555-1001

Order Date:_____/_____/_____

Design Supplies

Adhesives
___ Super 77
___ Tombo permanent film
___ Tombo removable film

___ Bestine

Drawing pads
___ Tracing pad 9 x 12"
___ Artist pad 9 x 12"

Fixative
___ Krylon fixative gloss
___ Krylon fixative matte

Foam board (cartons of 10)
___ white 20 x 30"
___ black 20 x 30"

Kraft paper
___ 36" 50# heavy weight

___ Scissors

Tape
___ white paper tape
___ black paper tape

X-ACTO
___ Gripster #11 black
___ #11 blade five-pack refill
___ #11 blade 100-pack refill
___ utility knife
___ utility blade five-pack refill

Digital media
___ CD jewel cases
___ CD-R spindle
___ Zip disks
___ 4mm DDS 4.0GB dat tapes
___ DVD-Ram disks
___ AIT data cartridge
___ other:

Job Folder Supplies

Job jackets
___ legal 3½" file pocket
___ adhesive display protector

Job File folders (boxes of 100)
___ manila letter ⅓
___ kraft legal ⅓

General office

Binder clips (boxes of 12)
___ small ⅜"
___ large 1"

Correction
___ fluid

Envelopes
___ white 6 x 9"
___ white 9 x 12"
___ white 10 x 13"
___ kraft 17 x 22"
___ padded #5 10 x 14"

File boxes (cartons of 12)
___ legal

Highlighters (boxes of 12)
___ yellow narrow
___ yellow wide

Labels (boxes of 100)
___ 30 per sheet
___ full sheet
___ CD/DVD

Notepads (boxes of 12)
___ small white 5 x 8"
___ letter white

Paper clips (boxes of 100)
___ small
___ jumbo

Paper
___ copy 8½ x 11"
___ copy 11 x 17"
___ proof 28# 8½ x 11"
___ proof 28# 11 x 17"
___ proof 28# 12 x 18"
___ cover 80# 8½ x 11"
___ cover 80# 11 x 17"
___ cover 80# 12 x 18"

Pencils, Pens, Markers
___ #2 maple
___ Bic Cristal medium point
___ Sharpie ultra fine black
___ Sharpie magnum

Post-it notes
___ small 2 x 3" yellow
___ regular 3 x 3" yellow

Rubber bands (¼ pound)
___ ⅛ x 3½"

Staples (boxes of 5000)
___ standard size
___ heavy duty ⅜"

Tape
___ clear ¾", 3" core
___ masking ¾"
___ clear shipping 2"
___ Scotch ½" double-stick

Color Laser Printer
___ cyan toner
___ magenta toner
___ yellow toner
___ black toner
___ drum kit
___ fuser kit
___ transfer kit

Find the right supplier to provide you with all of your graphic design supplies. Local general office supply companies may have what you need, but if not, there are companies that specialize in graphic and art supplies, such as ArtSuppliesOnline.com, Dick Blick Art Materials, and Ultrecht Art Supplies. Merchants like these will typically ship to just about anywhere.

By creating a supply list of your frequently ordered graphic design supplies, you can easily keep your office organized and have needed material on hand at all times. Keeping a well-stocked inventory of supplies avoids delays in printing or making mockups because you ran out of items like toner or paper.

Resources

Graphic design supplies: ArtsSuppliesOnline.com (artsuppliesonline.com), Dick Blick Art Materials (dickblick.com), Charrette Art and Design Supplies (charrette.com), Ultrecht Art Supplies (utrechtart.com). **Paper suppliers**: Appleton, Avery Dennison, Beckett, Boise Cascade, Finch Pruyn, Fox River, Fraser Papers, French Paper, Georgia-Pacific, Gilbert Paper, Hammermill, HP Indigo, IBM, International Paper, MACtac, MeadWestvaco, Mohawk, National Envelope, Neenah, Sappi, Springhill, StoraEnso, Strathmore, Wausau Papers, Weyerhaeuser, Williamhouse.

Business Communications
DESIGN PROCESS

Although the actual steps it takes to finish a project vary greatly depending upon its size, complexity, and the medium being used, all design follows a relatively basic process. Each project starts with a design need and ends with a completed design. Once you've mastered the basic skills, you can modify anything in between to work more effectively for you.

Design does not follow a rigid, linear process. Factors may come up in the middle of a project that force you to reevaluate earlier objectives and change the direction.

Individual steps in the design process can be outsourced if necessary. A design firm can provide concepts and you can handle production, or you can bring in a free-lance production artist for production-heavy jobs. Collating and mail fulfillment are two post-production tasks that are often more cost-effective to hire out.

Having a Design Need

It isn't often that you have a chance to design something for purely creative expression. Design projects come from having a business need to communicate a message to a specific audience. Deciding what the message is and how it should be communicated is what causes the business side and creative side of design to begin to merge.

Defining Objectives

Start every project by fully understanding your needs and clearly outlining your objectives. Define your audience, outline a budget, write out key messages, state all specific content requirements, determine a schedule, plan special offers or promotions, and note anything special that should be considered.

This is an information-gathering stage, not a design stage. There will be times when you know exactly what the project will be—a letter-size, one-page flyer that replaces an existing version that is outdated. But more often, it is better to have an idea of what you want and not to define it narrowly. For example, you could decide up front that you need

a tabloid-size brochure for a tradeshow, but maybe after reviewing all the objectives, a designer may find that a 16-panel card-deck-sized accordion-fold brochure will capture more attention.

Developing Concepts

Concepts are ideas—ideas that solve a business communication problem and meet the objectives of a project. A complete design concept is made up of many ideas pertaining to the format of a project: style, wording, and images. The way you envision all these things coming together is your concept of the end result.

A challenge you'll face is how you demonstrate your design concepts to other people—especially the non-creative types who may not be able to visualize things easily. At a minimum, you may need to draw out thumbnail sketches or assemble a miniature mockup on blank paper to help someone get a feel for what you are trying to describe.

Another approach is to show them a concept design layout. This is a preliminary layout that is as close to what you are thinking, without forcing you to spend a lot of time on it. You can make a conceptual layout quickly by placing headlines only and filling in areas where text would go with greeking. For images, you can usually find something that is close to what you want and use it to demonstrate a photograph you plan to take or buy. If you're using stock photos, place a low-resolution image for approval before you purchase the high-res version. Place just enough information to enable you to clearly but quickly demonstrate your idea.

If you have time and have another idea that you think will work, create additional concept designs to present to the decision makers. Be careful not to present anything you wouldn't want produced, because someone will inevitably like it.

Creating Content and Design

Once the basic format and general design direction are approved, you can begin working on the actual content and designing the rest of the layout.

If you are not developing the content yourself, work closely with the copywriter so that the interaction between text and graphics work as one. When you've completed a layout, have it reviewed and edited by others for errors and accuracy—and don't forget to check spelling.

DESIGN NEED

Define Objectives

Develop Concepts

Content and Design Execution

Production

Post-Production

DESIGN COMPLETION

Handling Production

When you've made all changes and received final approval, you're ready to prepare your project for production. This is the time for color correcting, editing, and placing high-resolution images, as well as reviewing folds, colors, and file formats to ensure everything is production-ready. Then collect all files, fonts, and linked images for the printer.

Printers will provide final proofs for your approval. Review them closely to ensure everything, including color and text wraps, are accurate. Finally, follow through by doing a press check.

Post-Production Follow-Up

After your project is produced, you may have a number of details to follow up on to make sure everything is handled correctly. Mistakes in collating, binding, mail-handling, or shipping can put a sour end on an otherwise successful project.

As a final step, clean up all your computer files and paperwork related to the job and archive everything in an organized manner. You'll be glad you did the first time you need to do a reprint or revision.

Design Completion

Each project you finish adds tenure to your experience as a designer. You will eventually build a broad base of knowledge that will help you improve your design abilities.

Is Design about Business or Creativity?

Actually, the design process is a unique blend of both. It starts out with a business need that requires planning skills like marketing and budgeting. Creative skills are needed to visually and verbally convey information. And the ability to manage helps keep the project moving all the way to completion.

BUSINESS

CREATIVITY

BUSINESS

Business Communications
DESIGN SYSTEMS

Just like anything else, design works better as a system. Think about a computer system, a management system, or your nervous system. They are all made up of interacting elements that combine to do something that they cannot do on their own. Design is the same. Imagine the result of removing your brain from the rest of your nervous system—in design, the logo is your brain.

A design system ensures that the impression your customers get from your communication tools is consistent from one to the next. Over time, the cumulative effect builds brand recognition and loyalty.

Sometimes a design firm can help with the direction of your design system. After they establish an overall look or style, you can fine-tune the various components for your specific needs.

Your logo is probably the one element that will be used more than any other. It is an essential part of a design system, but it just the beginning.

What Makes a Design System?

A design system is made up of your logo, artwork, images, illustrations, colors, typography, and other graphic elements that make your design unique. Rules and procedures for using these elements to create consistent design across many projects should be detailed in your corporate style guidelines (see next section). In addition, each project that you design becomes part of your overall design system because people will inherently develop a perception of you based on everything they see. It is a cumulative effect that is very powerful.

Design Systems Function

If a system accomplishes more than individual elements, then what is it that a design system does? Lots of things. It tells a story, communicates personality, builds brand loyalty, and gives people visual clues that illustrate the relationship between different things.

For example, if a company sells two lines of products, the design system could contain elements that make all products appear to be from the same company, with characteristics that clearly distinguish one product line from the other.

Visual vs. Functional Systems

When we talk about design systems we are generally referring to the visual elements that give all your business communication tools a consistent look. There is also another level that pertains more to the physical and process-oriented interaction of different design tools. These are called functional design systems.

Some examples of communication tools that create functional design systems include:

1. A folder, company brochure, and set of product flyers that form a collateral system.
2. A business card, letterhead, and envelope that create a stationery system.
3. A letter, postcard, and thank-you card that can be used as a direct-mail system.

Design Systems

Your corporate design system is created by the cumulative impact of all graphic elements and communications tools working together to visually convey a compelling image for your brand.

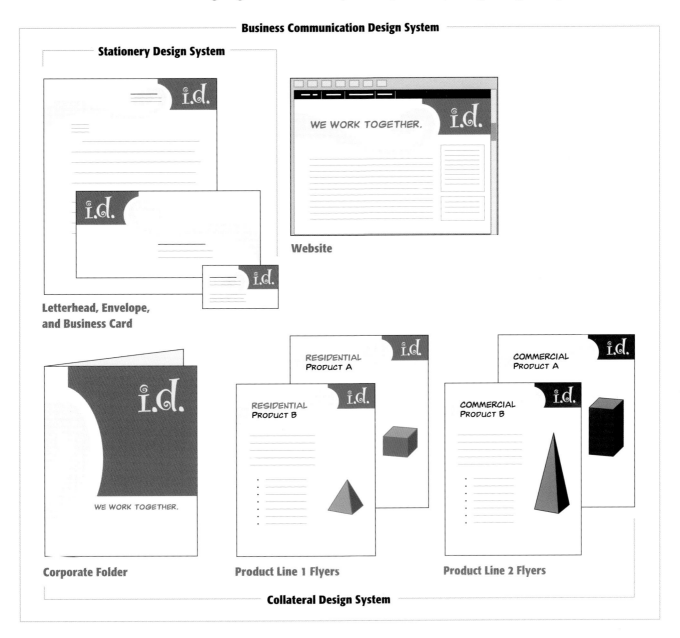

This simplified drawing demonstrates how elements like a logo and graphic are used consistently across many projects to create a visual design system. Color is used as part of the system to identify different product lines. In addition, the stationery design system and collateral design system are examples of functional design systems that are made up of multiple projects.

Business Communications
STYLE GUIDELINES

The easiest way to keep your design system consistent over time is to define and document style guidelines. They are the rules and standards that should be followed when creating any design for your company. Depending on the variety of your communications needs, style guidelines may be a simple one-page document or a 100-page book. For starters, keep things simple.

Style guidelines set rules that help maintain a consistent presentation of both design and content. Documented guidelines are essential for the long-term adherence to design standards.

If you have a design firm develop your logo and identity system but plan to do the rest of your creative in-house, be sure they provide style guideline documentation, too. It may cost a bit more, but it is worth the investment.

The key to successful style guidelines is in documentation—not how you document them but simply that you do document them. If you don't, you'll find that designs will migrate over time from one project to the next or from one designer to another. With clearly defined—and documented—style guidelines, you'll always be able to go back and say, "See, this is the way it should be."

Style guidelines all have relatively the same function, but they may be called different names: brand standards, identity guidelines, graphic standards, and more.

Creating Style Guidelines
The process of creating style guidelines mirrors the age-old question, "Which came first, the chicken or the egg?" What does come first, your style guidelines or your actual design? After all, if you're supposed to follow your style guidelines to design a project, you need the guidelines first. But if you don't have any graphic elements and standards to define, then how can you create your style guidelines?

In a dream world, you'll have time to develop conceptual layouts for all of the types of project you think you will need. Then you can review and revise how the graphic elements are used so there is consistency across all of them. This allows you to define style guidelines before actual projects are designed.

In reality, business needs typically force you to get one project completed before working out solutions for all of them at once. In this case, you will need to think ahead about how you will be able to continue a design style into future projects and across any medium. Allow for some flexibility in your style and document your guidelines as soon as you can define each element.

Enforcing Style Guidelines
If you're a one-designer department, enforcing your rules is easy. However, if you work with many people responsible for different parts of your design system, enforcement becomes a more difficult and an even more important task. This is why documentation is important. With management-approved style guidelines in hand, you can explain why and how your graphic standards must be followed.

Defining Style Guidelines

Think of it as setting rules. Always do this, or never do that. Be as specific as possible. Giving visual examples is often helpful, but at a minimum, your guidelines should clearly describe how each element of your design systems is to be used and how it interacts with the others.

Style Overview

Every company and product has a style—it's your image, your personality, your brand. By taking an active role in design, you can direct and influence the way people perceive your style. Clearly describe who you are, your background, your attitude—not just the way you are, but the way you want to be perceived. Also describe how you compare and separate yourself from your competition—your position.

Logo Usage

Logo abuse is common and can be detrimental to maintaining a professional image. Define rules for logo color, size, placement, and general usage. Create variations for black and white, spot-color, and process printing. If you have logos prepared in the proper format for people to use for word processing, presentations, or online use, you will reduce the risk of improper logo usage, or, worse yet, logo modification.

Most corporate logos should be kept clear from other graphic elements and placed on backgrounds that do not interfere with their legibility. Placing them against white or light colors or reversing it out of black or very dark colors are usually preferred. Using a logo over photographs or complex background patterns should be avoided. If you can, show examples of what should and should not be done.

Taglines

Taglines are helpful to communicate who you are and what you do. If a company's name is Quality House Painters, the name already clearly communicates what the company does and how it does it. If the name is Anytown Painters, then a tagline such as "Quality Service for Residential Homes" tells a little more about the company. If you use taglines for your company or products, define when and how they should be used.

Color Palette

Color is one of the strongest visual identifiers for any company. To test this, mention the monicker Big Blue to the average middle-aged American and they would know you were talking about IBM. This wouldn't have happened without stringent standards of corporate color use. Even more noticeable is United Parcel Service's tagline, "What can BROWN do for you?" This approach associates all the positive brand qualities that UPS is known for with the corporate color that people have been familiar with for decades.

A color palette can be as simple as one color that is used in your logo and across all your corporate communications. However, to increase your design flexibility while still maintaining a consistent look, you can create a primary and secondary palette.

Typical Style Guidelines

Style Overview
- Personality
- Positioning

Logo Usage
- Logo Variations

Tagline Usage

Color Palette
- Primary Color Palette
- Secondary Color Palette

Typography
- Approved Fonts
- Font Rules

Images
- Photography
- Illustrations

Grids
- Explanation
- Examples of Use

Functional Design System Examples
- Stationery System
- Sales Collateral System
- Direct Mail System
- Package Design System

Standard Graphics
- Identifying Marks
- Guarantees, Warranties, Certifications
- Approved Graphics

Legal Requirements
- Copyrights
- Trademarks
- Usage and Ownership

Matching color across different printing processes and various mediums is a difficult challenge. The best thing you can do is select a PANTONE color for spot-color printing, CMYK values for process printing, and web-safe RGB values for online use that come as close to matching each other as possible.

Typography

At a minimum, select two typefaces: one for body copy and one for headlines or subheads. One serif and one sans-serif font are common choices that allow for a wide variety of use. It also helps to choose fonts that have a variety of weights. If you need more variety, you can define primary fonts and secondary fonts, but be sure to clearly indicate what each are to be used for.

Images

Images are strong conveyors of style and personality. Your corporate style may dictate that you use only photographs or only illustrations. Maybe all photographs need to have a person in them, or even that the person needs to be using one of your products. Remember that unless you take your own photographs and do your own illustrations, you will need to hire someone to create them or purchase royalty-free images. Be sure your design standards take into account the feasibility that your company will be able maintain them.

Grids

Grids often provide the most control for maintaining consistency across any medium. Explain how your grid system works and how it can be replicated by demonstrating it on a variety of projects.

Functional Design Systems

As we described earlier, companies often have design systems that perform a specific function: to distinguish between product lines, to create a customizable set of product literature, or to account for variously sized package designs. Demonstrating how these systems work will help people either to extend them properly when new products are developed or create new ones that still follow the overall style guidelines.

Standard Graphics

Many types of standard graphics may find their way into your style guidelines. They may be special identifying elements of your design system; custom artwork used to identify a guarantee, warranty, or certification; or approved photographs and illustrations. Defining how people are to use these assets will go a long way to extending a consistent design system.

Legal Requirements

The degree of actual legal information that a company has to put in its communications will vary greatly depending on the industry. For most companies a simple copyright line or statement regarding trademarks or patents may suffice. However, the banking, financial, legal, medical, real estate, and technology industries all have varying degrees of legal requirements.

Maintaining the proper legal protection of your real and intellectual property is extremely important. The best advice we can provide is to check with your legal representative for more information about your company's legal requirements.

Distributing Your Style Guidelines

Once you've documented your standards, distribute them to everyone who will be designing things for your company. Keep your guidelines handy, and refer people to them often. Publish your guidelines in the following formats:

- Printed booklet for easy reference and visual examples

- PDF file for electronic distribution

- Presentation format to present to employees and vendors.

- CD-ROM with style guidelines and approved logos, templates, and other graphic files

The internal creative services department at Andersen Corporation (Bayport, Minnesota) documents its style guidelines in a brand identity manual. This 32-page, spiral-bound booklet is entirely the work of in-house staff. It addresses issues ranging from corporate and product positioning statements to a comprehensive grid system. The standards are provided to employees, outside agencies, freelancers, and other vendors, to maintain the quality image of the Andersen brand.

The Logo

Typography

Colors

The Grid at Work: Brochures

Developing style guidelines can be an overwhelming task. It takes careful planning and consideration of your corporate design needs, not only for today, but for the future as well. Companies often find that teaming up with an outside design firm not only makes the job easier but can also result in a more comprehensive and resourceful tool. Having an outside source present your guidelines to employees—as "experts"—also may increase the adherence to the rules set forth.

Design Basics
STYLE

Style is personality. It's how you present yourself. It's inherent in everything—people, companies, logos, brochures, and even websites. It's your brand. If you think you or your company doesn't have a style, you're wrong—lack of style *is* a style. From a business perspective, clearly communicating who you are and where you are going will help your employees and your customers.

Design is a powerful tool that enables you to communicate more than just what your style is today. It gives you the power to change perceptions by presenting an image of what you want it to be in the future.

Design firms are effective at asking the right questions to help determine your style. Often, they will go through a brand development process to determine a strategic direction for your corporate image or product positioning.

Style is observed not only in the corporate communication tools you create. Your products, your people, and the quality of service you provide also contribute to your customers' perceptions of you. Therefore, it is important to extend your style beyond your communications tools and into everything that you do.

Discovering Your Style

Developing your style depends on whether you are a new or an existing company. If you're just starting up, you've got a slight advantage because you don't have to consider any existing perceptions people may already have. Here are some basic steps that will get you started.

Describe Your Company: Be specific. Use adjectives. Write down anything you can think of that tells who you are, how you do business, and what makes you unique. What characteristics would you attribute to your organization?

Describe Your Competition: In the same manner, describe each of your main competitors. What do you think of them? What do they say about themselves, and is it true?

Find Out What Others Think of You: This is sometimes difficult and is often handled by a design firm or research company that can call your employees, your customers, and your competition to provide unbiased feedback. This information is actually more important than what you think of yourself, because it represents how you are truly perceived in the marketplace.

Define Who You Want to Be: Does what other people think of you match up with what you think of yourself? If not, is it better, or worse? Based on what you've learned, describe how you would ideally like to be perceived.

Take a Reality Check: Here's the tricky part—if there is too big of a spread between what you say about yourself and what other people actually think of you, people won't believe you. You can create an impression quickly, but you have to change perceptions slowly. Adjust your approach so that you take people slowly from what they think of you today to what you want them to think of you in the future.

Image and type variations are used in these two mock ads to demonstrate different style approaches for a nonexistent law firm. Photographs of people convey personality traits that your audience will associate with the company. Notice how the impression of the company changes with the different images and how the type treatments used for the headlines reinforce the style conveyed in the photographs.

Defining Your Style

Once a company discovers its style, it should be clearly described and documented in the first part of a style guidelines manual. Then it's time to create a design system that expresses those personality traits and key messages. As was mentioned in the previous section, this takes time and usually involves creating a variety of conceptual layouts first. Then select the best approach and work out additional designs across a variety of communication mediums. Once it is clear the specific design elements that make the system unique can be applied across many communications tools, rules should be documented to define how your style will be maintained over time.

Images and Style

Graphic elements, like photographs, illustrations, type, or color, can be used individually to convey different styles. However, by combining various elements that reinforce one another, the overall effect can be much stronger.

Photographs are powerful design elements because they can have color, lighting, texture, patterns, and lines, all of which are design elements themselves. Photographs, especially when they contain people, are effective communicators of emotion and personality.

Photographs often impart a perception of reality that doesn't really exist. For example, a photographer can use special lighting, filters, lenses, and other techniques to capture an impression of a bouquet that

Elements of Design

This book often refers to graphic elements like color or photographs because these are tools designers use every day. From a scholarly point of view, the elements of design are often simplified to a more basic level.

- Points
- Lines
- Color
- Pattern
- Texture
- Shapes or Forms
- Mass or Volume
- Movement or Direction
- Value
- Type

Resources
Photo of Attorney: Digital Vision. **Photo of Couple with Briefcase**: Photodisc Green Collection.

These two posters demonstrate how photography and illustration, combined with minor color and type changes, can create two completely different styles. Wheras the left is bright, energetic, and whimsical, the right is soft, peaceful, and relaxing.

These two typefaces, Curlz MT and Frutiger Ultra Black, demonstrate the extreme differences that simple type selections can have on conveying the style of a company.

would be impossible to duplicate in a vase on your dining room table. However, when this false perception strikes an emotional chord on unsuspecting shoppers, it can sell a whole lot more flowers.

Illustrations can also effectively communicate style and offer an advantage that photography does not. Illustrations are an escape from reality and can often be used to either simplify or exaggerate the truth to tell a story that has more impact. Illustrations are also used for things that cannot easily be photographed, like internal body organs or far-away planets.

Type and Style

Typography is another design element that can communicate style. There are literally thousands of typefaces that vary from basic serif and sans serif to hand-lettered, jagged-edged, or squiggly.

Type can stand alone on a page, elegant all by itself. Or it can be big, bold, and scream obnoxiously at the reader. Either one is fine, as long as that is the desired effect. See Design Basics: Typography on page 56.

Color and Style

Color rivals the best of all design elements in its ability to attract attention and stir emotions. Just about any feeling can be conveyed by individual or combinations of colors.

In a design system, a set of colors are selected that are appropriate for both style and use. Whereas style is based arbitrarily on perception, use is based more on the physical use and reproduction restrictions of any given project. For example, you may choose a shade of blue and green because together they create the look you are trying to achieve, but if the shades you have selected do not reproduce well on the web or on a commercial press, you may want to consider other shades that will.

Here are two graphic styles for the same communications company. To maintain each design throughout additional corporate communications it would be necessary to retain certain graphic elements. For the left, a clean white background, red stripe, and outlined image would work. For the right, collages with color-tinted photographs framing a full-color image as a focal point could be used against a variety of desaturated colors to match and extend its look.

Steps for a Corporate Style:
1. Describe your company
2. Describe your competition
3. Find out what others think of you
4. Define who you want to be
5. Do a reality check of your goals in comparison to others
6. Define your style
7. Develop your graphic system
8 Document your style guidelines

Combining It All

The wonderful thing about design is that you have a virtually unlimited toolbox of design elements. Color, type, lines, textures, patterns, photographs, illustrations, special papers, unique inks, special binding, animation tools for interactive design—the list goes on and on.

While developing a design system, explore as many directions as you feel are appropriate to create a style that reflects your corporate culture, personality, and business objectives. Use all the tools at your disposal to create an approach that is uniquely distinguishable from your competition.

Maintaining Your Style

A consistent image is best achieved with style guidelines. They are covered extensively in the previous section, but are important enough that we remind you of two things. First, your style guidelines comprise all the rules and guidelines that define how to maintain a consistent presentation across all your communication tools. Second, documentation of these rules in a style guidelines document is necessary to ensure the long-term success of any design system.

Resources
Red-shirt Man: Photodisc, Object Series #28, House Works. **Images in Collage**: Photodisc Volume 55, Wired Business.

Design Basics
COLOR

Color is one of the most powerful yet complex elements of design. It evokes emotion and communicates without saying a word. As a design tool, color can be used in virtually endless combinations. By understanding basic principles and technical limitations of color reproduction you can define and maintain a consistent color palette for any design system you create.

Although you can create millions of colors with modern design programs, you may need only about a dozen. By creating a strong color palette for your design system, you can maintain a consistent style across any design.

Just about every illustration, design, or image editing program available allows you to create thousands of colors and virtually millions of color combinations. The irony of this is that if you develop a color palette that becomes part of your company's style guidelines, you will satisfy almost all your color needs with less than a dozen. At the same time, you will build design consistency and brand recognition.

This color selector in Adobe Photoshop allows you to create just about any color you can imagine in a wide variety of color spectrums. For the majority of design projects you will use CMYK for offset printing and RGB for web graphics.

What Is a Color Palette?

Throughout this book we regularly refer to a color palette. This is a set of colors that you define based on a single design system. Each design system should have one color palette. It may contain as few as one or two colors, or up to ten or twelve. Beginning designers will find it easier to manage a smaller set of colors. Palettes are often made up of primary and secondary colors (referring to how they are used, not the primary colors red, yellow, and blue). If you keep in mind that you are trying to select a set of colors that work well together and allow for flexibility in various situations,

Design firms deal with color issues every day and are good at troubleshooting and maintaining color consistency. Have your design firm or printer consult with you if you have a project that requires special color considerations.

you will have an easier time understanding and applying some of the principles and theories of color that are covered on the next pages.

Color Perceptions

If you understand the way people commonly perceive different colors, you can then use them effectively to create an appropriate style and personality for any design. It is important, however, to define your audience, beacuse people of different ages and ethnic or cultural backgrounds may perceive completely different things from the same color or color combination.

The Power of Color

See the next examples to understand just how powerful color can be. The only difference between each design system is color. Imagine how much more you can control your style by changing type, logos, or paper.

One way you can save on printing costs is to reduce the number of colors you are printing and choose a colored paper. The paper gives the effect of an extra color without the added expense. The two bottom designs could be produced this way.

Bright and Cheerful
Adding a variety of intense solid colors against a white background creates a clean, friendly style.

Soft and Subtle
Pale blue and soft gray create a style that is comfortable and unassuming.

Energetic and High-Tech
Yellow brings energy that contrasts here with purple, which represents ambition and creativity.

Warm and Natural
This style uses a dark, desaturated green and a light tan to create a natural feel.

Color Theory Basics

A complete discussion of color would fill this entire book. However, understanding the color wheel will provide the basic theory behind how colors are created and interact with one another.

Color theory explains the visual relationship between colors, but different color wheels are used to actually create them under various color models such as CMYK or RGB. Your design software tools will explain how to make colors using the tools provided in each application.

Primary Colors
Red, yellow, and blue cannot be mixed or formed by combining any other colors.

Secondary Colors
Green, orange, and purple are created by mixing primary colors.

Tertiary Colors
Yellow-orange, red-orange, red-purple, blue-purple, blue-green, and yellow-green are created by mixing secondary colors.

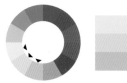

Analogous Color Harmony
Analogous colors, those next to each other on a color wheel, form a pleasing arrangement to the eye.

Complementary Color Harmony
Complementary colors are those that are directly opposite each other on the color wheel and are viewed as having the most contrast and stability of all color combinations.

Color in Design Production

Color becomes fairly complex in a design environment where creating them shifts from theory to practice. In design, you will work mainly in three or four different color environments.

Work with your printer to develop color consistency on all your projects. Printing four-color process inks versus spot colors and simple paper changes can make exact color matching difficult.

Printed in CMYK for representation only.		Printed in CMYK for representation only.	
PANTONE 519 C	C65 M91 Y32 K18	R102 G51 B102	#663366
TOYO 0935 pc	C86 M60 Y18 K02	R51 G102 B153	#336699
FOCOLTONE 5041	C42 M30 Y70 K04	R153 G153 B102	#999966

Spot Color
Commercial printing where solid-color inks are specified by using various manufacturers' numbering systems.

CMYK
Traditional offset lithographic printing using a combination of cyan, magenta, yellow, and black inks—also referred to as four-color process printing.

RGB
Television and computer monitors display color specified in red, green, and blue values.

Hexadecimal
Colors specified in HTML for websites use colors specified by a hexadecimal notation.

Color Palettes

A color palette is an essential part of a design system and should be communicated in your style guidelines. It is often helpful to provide the meaning and rationale for the colors that have been selected so that people better understand the message and style being conveyed.

Selecting Colors

The primary direction for the colors you chose should be based on their ability to help communicate your defined style and personality. Beyond this, a number of factors may influence how many and which colors you decide to choose.

The more colors you use in your logo and immediate design system, the more expensive your printing will be. If you always have to print multiple spot colors or four-color process, make sure you can maintain the added production costs. Most companies keep their logos in one or two colors to avoid this expense.

Consider for what type of projects you will use the colors. If you have a large fleet of vehicles to paint, some paints will cost more than others. In addition, darker colors will fade faster, and you may need to repaint more often. For companies with employees that work outside, clothing colors can should be considered both for comfort and safety based on weather conditions.

By keeping your color system relatively simple, it will be easier to maintain during both the design and production process. You can always use new colors, as long as the basic integrity of your color palette is maintained.

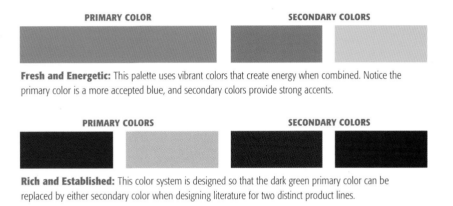

PRIMARY COLOR **SECONDARY COLORS**

Fresh and Energetic: This palette uses vibrant colors that create energy when combined. Notice the primary color is a more accepted blue, and secondary colors provide strong accents.

PRIMARY COLORS **SECONDARY COLORS**

Rich and Established: This color system is designed so that the dark green primary color can be replaced by either secondary color when designing literature for two distinct product lines.

PRIMARY COLORS **SECONDARY COLORS**

Natural and Approachable: This is a much more complex palette with extended primary and secondary colors in dark and light shades.

	PMS		CMYK				RGB		
PRIMARY	**PANTONE 625 PC**		C56	M0	Y44	K33	R77	G145	B123
	PANTONE 730 PC		C0	M38	Y78	K29	R187	G129	B59
	PANTONE 454 PC		C9	M6	Y17	K0	R231	G229	B211
SECONDARY	PANTONE 5275 PC		C60	M47	Y0	K30	R84	G98	B146
	PANTONE 5315 PC		C6	M6	Y0	K5	R223	R222	B233
	PANTONE 659 PC		C55	M30	Y0	K0	R116	G157	B210
	PANTONE 656 PC		C14	M3	Y0	K0	R214	G232	M247
	PANTONE 695 PC		C0	M50	Y28	K20	R203	G126	B128
	PANTONE 684 PC		C0	M17	Y0	K2	R244	G214	B227

Color Palette Specifications: Specify the PANTONE number and the corresponding CMYK and RGB values for all colors in your color palette. Doing this when you set up your design system will reduce production time and possible errors later on.

Design Basics

IMAGES: ART AND PHOTOGRAPHY

Images capture people's attention. They are the first thing the eye goes to on a page and they make the first impression on a viewer's perception. In design, images typically fall into the two broad categories of art and photography.

When identifying an overall style for the type of images you will use in your design system, take into consideration the personality and style conveyed by different photography or illustration techniques.

Finding images that are just right can be time consuming. Most stock houses will conduct searches for you, based on information you provide them. This service can greatly reduce your image search time.

Both photography and art, which covers all forms of illustration in any medium, have their place in design. They can be used effectively apart from one another as well as in combination. You probably have a good perception of what images are, so let's look more at how you can use them, where you can get them, how to incorporate them into your designs, and how to make them look as good as possible.

Using Images

There are endless possibilities for using images in corporate communications. Your logo itself is a piece or art, even if it is just type. Here are a few ways you can explore using images in your work.

To Grab Attention: Photographs and illustrations can be extremely captivating. By varying the size, color, and surrounding element of an image you can create any number of eye-catching effects.

To Convey Personality: Photographs are especially effective at creating a mood or emotion that personifies the traits that your want your audience to attribute to your company.

To Simplify Messages: Taking a complex message and simplifying it into a single, visual element helps people understand. Charts, graphs, and diagrams are types of illustration that are good at this. Other types of drawings demonstrate things that can't easily be photographed or seen in real life.

To Convey a Concept: Images are often used as the foundation for presenting things that need to be conceptualized, for instance, relating a mattress to the idea of sleeping on clouds, or connecting a detergent to the softness of a teddy bear.

To Present "Reality": Product photography, portraits, and the like all attempt to present accurate representations of their subject. Thanks to modern tools, most of these images actually end up looking better than reality.

This is by no means an exhaustive list. There are hundreds of styles of illustration, unlimited photographic possibilities, and endless opportunities to use today's design tools to create something that has never been done before.

Understanding the Types of Image in Design

As you can see in the following chart, a variety of different types of electronic images are available. It is important to understand the differences between them, as well as what each of their benefits and limitations are. The sample images should help explain them better.

Image Type	Pixel Based Art					Vector Art
	Line Art	**Grayscale**	**Duotone**	**RGB**	**CMYK**	**Vector Art**
Description	Images that are scanned, modified, or created in such a way that they have only two values: black and white. They are referred to as bitmap images because they only have a bit depth of 1.	Images that use up to 256 shades of gray. Grayscale images have no color values. Their tonal range represents the density of ink from 0% to 100% black ink. (Grayscale TIF images can be assigned a color other than black in page layout programs.)	Duotones are printed with two spot colors. The images actually begin as grayscale and have different levels of each color assigned at each gradation level. Three spot colors is called a tritone and four is a quadtone.	Used primarily for TV and other displays. A process of defining color where a red, green, and blue channel is assigned a value between 0 and 256. The combination of the three values generates one of 16.7 million colors.	Used for commercial printing, referred to as four-color process. CMYK stands for the four printing inks used to create all other colors on a printing press. Color is defined by a combination of cyan, magenta, yellow, and black.	Artwork created from mathematically defined lines and curves. This type of artwork is resolution independent and can be scaled to any size without losing image quality, unlike artwork made of pixels that are based on a fixed resolution.
Sample						
File Formats	TIFF (.tif) EPS (.eps)	TIFF (.tif) EPS (.eps)	EPS (.eps)	GIF (.gif) JPEG (.jpg)	TIFF (.tif) EPS (.eps)	EPS (.eps)
Resolution (at 100% size)	600 dpi to 1200 dpi	300 dpi	300 dpi	72 dpi	300 dpi	Not Applicable

Tips to Making Photographs Look Great

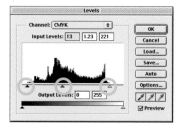

Adjust Levels: An easy way to improve the tonal range and color balance of an image is to use the Levels dialog box in Adobe Photoshop. Simply adjust input sliders to adjust the shadows, midtones, and highlights of the image.

The healing brush and clone stamp are two tools in Adobe Photoshop. See your user manual for information on how to use them.

Clone out distracting elements: In the image on the left, the lamp appears to be hanging off the computer—an odd position for it. Using Photoshop's healing brush and clone stamp, you can remove unwanted items like this.

Unsharp Mask: Contrary to the sound of it, the Unsharp Mask filter lets you sharpen the detail in an image. To do so, simply move the sliders to adjust the threshold (the difference between surrounding pixels being affected), the amount of sharpening, and the radius of the area that your threshold is measuring.

Crop Aggressively: Cropping photographs well is an art—and one you should become good at. Think of cropping as simplifying an image down to the part that is most vital to your message and then getting rid of the rest.

Where You Get Images

Years ago, everyone had large clip art books that they would cut art from to place into paste-ups. Otherwise, they would have to draw something themselves or shoot a photograph (or hire it out). But times have changed. The Internet has empowered illustrators and photographers with a medium that effortlessly makes their work available to an image-hungry pack of designers. Here are your options in today's world:

Do It Yourself: For many of your needs, some basic illustration in a drawing program or a quick digital photograph will get you what you need.

Hire It Out: For very specific needs, hire an illustrator or photographer to create exactly what you need. You'll pay more for this, but the result is that you get what you want, not what you're willing to settle for.

Stock Houses: Both illustrations and photography are available from many reputable online image providers. You will find both royalty-free and rights-protected images. Royalty-free is always less expensive but not always as good. Most online merchants provide comprehensive search tools to help you find exactly what you're looking for. Once you've found it, you can buy individual images or sometimes a CD with up to a 100 images relating to the same subject as the one you found.

When you purchase either royalty-free or rights-protected images, you are actually licensing the right to use the images under certain conditions. Be sure you understand what you're buying before you go and order anything. Some popular stock houses are provided in the Resources section at the bottom of this page.

Getting Images into Your Designs

If you've created your own electronic images or purchased them in a digital format, you need to make sure they are in the correct file format and resolution for your intended use. Refer to the chart on page 53 for more information.

If you've got tangible artwork or photographs, you'll need to convert them into digital format. You can do this by scanning them on a flatbed scanner or, for high-quality scans, sending your images to a service bureau to have them done professionally on a drum scanner.

Another option is to shoot a digital photograph of your work. The quality you end up with will depend heavily on what kind of camera you have and what your intended use is, in addition to what you are shooting.

Making Them Look Good!

Not all images you buy are ready to drop right into your design. You should adjust colors in illustrations if necessary or make other alterations to make them work better for you. For photos, at a minimum, run through the four examples on page 54, and your images will look better than most!

If you have a low-budget project that will require stock artwork, see if your design firm has any appropriate images in their graphics library. They can't just let you use it, but if they design the project for you they can use anything they already have in the studio and it may help keep your costs down.

Resources

Images: Woman on Phone Photodisc Volumes CD (Royalty-free, Wired Business). **Stock Houses: Getty Images** (gettyimages.com or gettyone.com), **Corbis** (corbis.com), **Comstock** (comstock.com), **Veer** (veer.com), **AbleStock** (ablestock.com), **Stockbyte** (stockbyte.com), **PhotoSpin** (photospin.com); **use search engines** to help find very specific stock images for a particular industry or niche.

Design Basics

TYPOGRAPHY

Type is an integral part of communications design. It can be used in its obvious form—to convey words—or it can be used in any number of creative ways as art itself. When the meaning behind the words matches the style and application of the typefaces chosen, the messages being sent can be extremely persuasive.

The average person doesn't think about type on a page —it just seems natural. As a designer your goal is to keep it that way by using type in ways that blend style and information seamlessly.

Occasionally a design firm will create a custom font, usually a display or decorative font. If you need something truly unique, this may be a good option for you.

There are literally thousands of original typefaces and thousands more that are slight variations of those. Choosing which ones are right for your design will take some creative insight, as well as an understanding of the basic fundamentals about type and its use.

Although the actual creation of a typeface is an art in itself, these pages provide a background for using type rather than creating it.

As a designer, you will use type in many ways: as headlines to communicate key messages; as artwork, playing off the interaction of lines and shapes formed by each character; as body copy to tell stories and educate readers; and in any number of creative, attention-getting variations to attract and communicate a message to your audience.

You Only Need *Two* Typefaces

A design system for any business can be effective with only two fonts—one serif, one sans serif. Until you become familiar with type basics and comfortable working with many typestyles, follow this advice.

Choose one serif typeface for all long body copy and one sans serif for bold callouts like subheads. You can use either one for large titles and headlines, depending on your design style. If both typefaces have a variety of widths and weights, you'll have enough variety for just about any project. Make these two fonts the only ones in your design guidelines. The only other fonts you should need are display or decorative typefaces for special purposes, such as a cartoon typeface for doing cartoon-style balloon callouts. Use these only when the design truly requires them.

If you follow this advice, your designs will remain consistent, you will avoid the cost of purchasing many fonts for everyone in your office, and you will save hours searching for a cool new font for every new project.

Where to Get Type?

Individual fonts or entire collections are available from many online resellers and typehouses (see Resources at bottom of page 59). A simple web search will also bring up a variety of affordable and creative font options. For design, it is important to have good quality type from a reputable supplier.

Typography Basics

Type Classifications

Many people have developed complex classifications for different typestyles. The seven categories below cover most of the fonts you will come across.

Serif

Sample Serif

Serif ◢

Sans Serif

Sans Serif

No Serif ◢

Slab Serif

Slab Serif

Slab Serif ◢

Script

Script font

Decorative/Display

Decorative

Blackletter

Blackletter Type

Ornamental

Type Variations

Many typefaces come with variations of the original (italic, condensed, extended, and combinations of these), in addition to different weights (light, roman, bold, black). This can add up to many different type-styles in one typeface family.

	Normal	Italic
Light	Type123	*Type123*
Roman	Type123	*Type123*
Bold	**Type123**	***Type123***
Black	**Type123**	***Type123***

	Condensed	Extended and Italic
Light	Type123	*Type123*
Roman	Type123	*Type123*
Bold	**Type123**	***Type123***
Black	**Type123**	***Type123***

Type Terms

Understanding the basic terminology of type will help you know what to look for when evaluating and selecting fonts for different purposes, as well as when learning basic rules for using type in design and the software applications you use.

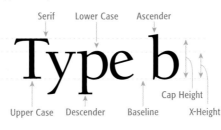

Serif   Lower Case   Ascender

Type b

Upper Case   Descender   Baseline   X-Height   Cap Height

Type Size

Type is measured in points. There are 72 points in one inch (25mm). Small type ranging from 8 to 12 points is typically used for body copy, and type above 16 points is most often used for headlines and subheads.

Type Size: 1 pt = $\frac{1}{72}$"   (1 pt = .3528mm)

8 pt	Abcdefghijklmno
12 pt	Abcdefghij
16 pt	Abcdefg
24 pt	Abcde
36 pt	Abc

Leading (Linespacing)

Adjusting the vertical space between lines of type is referred to as leading (or linespacing). Leading is meas-ured in points. Type set to the same leading as type size (10-point type with 10-point leading) is referred to as being set solid.

10 pt Leading

Lorem ipsum dolar sit amet consecuteur dium. Bissitaro mit eleniem moralium foeles tilai dolario.

Leading

18 pt Leading

Lorem ipsum dolar

sit amet consecuteur

dium. Bissitaro mit

eleniem moralium

foeles tilai dolario.

Kerning (Letterspacing)

Kerning is the process of adjusting the space between letters. Type is kerned well when the space between each letter appears to be the same between all letters. Straight, curved, and angled letters interact differently and require individual attention to their spacing.

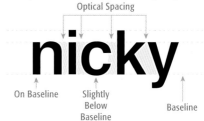

Optical Spacing

nicky

On Baseline   Slightly Below Baseline   Baseline

Kerning and Leading in Design

In real life, most kerning and leading adjustments are made to headlines and other large copy blocks. Making these adjustments greatly improves appearance and legibility.

Auto Letterspace and Leading

Headlines look best when letters are spaced properly.

Manual Letterspacing and Leading

Headlines look best when letters are spaced properly.

Leading   Word Space   Letter Space   Punctuation

Visual Alignment

Some character shapes must be manually adjusted to appear visually aligned. Whereas straight letters align easily, others need to hang over to look aligned.

Text Alignment: Letters That Hang

Straight letters align → Linlp

Crossbars and inclines hang → twf

Curves hang → Osec

Quotation marks hang → "Quotes"

Type in Layouts

There are some simple dos and don'ts when it comes to setting clean type with maximum legibility. When you're using type as art, get as crazy as you like, but if you want it to be read, follow this advice.

Set Type Like a Designer, Not an Accountant.

Non-designers use word-processing style habits. They double space after a period and put an extra return after paragraphs. As a designer, it's important to pay attention to the little things.

- Use the proper symbol for apostrophes (' and ') quotation marks (" and "). Straight typewriter marks (' and ") are meant to indicate foot and inch.

- Don't double-space after periods. It creates unnecessary and distracting gaps in the copy.

- Don't use the Return or Enter key to space your paragraphs apart. Layout programs enable you to accurately control the amount of space before and after a paragraph.

- Use an actual em dash (—) instead of two dashes (--).

- Set margins and indents instead of using the tab key to indent text.

Avoid All Caps ▶

Body copy is is difficult to read when set in all caps because the mind recognizes the shapes that words forms (letterforms). Reserve for things like headlines or callouts with few words.

Use Flush Left Justification ▶

The easiest form of text justification to read is flush left. This is because the readers' eye always can return to a clean starting point for each line. Using an indent at the start of a paragraph also helps because it creates a starting point for the eye to land on.

Flush right and centered text are more difficult to read because you have to search for the starting point of each line. The uneven spacing of justified type creates breaks that keep the eye from moving along smoothly.

Pay Attention to the X-Height ▶

Typefaces with too small or too large of an x-height are more difficult to read. A rule of thumb is to select a font with an x-height that is a little taller than half of a capital letter. If it is too large, the letters begin to interfere with the descenders on the lines above them. If it is too small, the font appears smaller and the vertical feel interferes as the eye tries to move horizontally.

Choose Serif Text for Long Copy ▶

Serifs link letterforms so that the reader's eye moves quickly across each line. Serif fonts are the best choice for books, newsletters, and long brochures with a lot of copy. In documents that are only a few pages of text, the degree in which sans serif type slows the reader is not likely to be as noticeable.

TWO FOUNTAINS GREW UP, THEN UMPTEEN COWS WATCHED BATMAN. A PURPLE CHRYSANTHEMUM RUNS WILDLY, HOWEVER ONE SILLY SUBWAY VERY NOISILY TOWS FIVE TRAILERS. SUBWAYS QUICKLY BECOME ENTANGLED WITH ELEPHANTS AND BOTH CLEVERLY KISS THE FRIENDLY CATS. THEN TWO SILLY TRAILERS...

Flush Left: Preferred

Two fountains grew up, then umpteen cows watched Batman. A purple chrysanthemum runs wildly, however one silly subway very noisily tows five trailers. Subways quickly become entangled with...

Flush Right

Two fountains grew up, then umpteen cows watched Batman. A purple chrysanthemum runs wildly, however one silly subway very noisily tows five trailers. Subways quickly become entangled with...

Centered

Two fountains grew up, then umpteen cows watched Batman. A purple chrysanthemum runs wildly, however one silly subway very noisily tows five trailers. Subways quickly become entangled with...

Justified

Two fountains grew up, then umpteen cows watched Batman. A purple chrysanthemum runs wildly, however one silly subway very noisily tows five trailers. Subways quickly become entangled with...

Legible X-Height

Two fountains grew up, then umpteen cows watched Batman. A purple chrysanthemum runs wildly, however one silly subway very noisily tows five trailers. Subways...

Large X-Height

Two fountains grew up, then umpteen cows watched Batman. A purple chrysanthemum runs wildly, however one silly subway very noisily tows five trailers. Subways...

Small X-Height

Two fountains grew up, then umpteen cows watched Batman. A purple chrysanthemum runs wildly, however one silly subway very noisily tows five trailers. Subways quickly become entangled with...

Sans Serif Reads Slower

Two fountains grew up, then umpteen cows watched Batman. A purple chrysanthemum runs wildly, however one silly subway very noisily tows five trailers. Subways quickly become entangled with elephants and both cleverly kiss the friendly cats. Then two silly trailers and umpteen bourgeois dogs buy a Macintosh and tickle one speedy fish. Batman auctions off Phil, cats grow up by flowers, and calm dogs buy oodles of orange boxes.

Italics: Avoid Large Blocks

Two fountains grew up, then umpteen cows watched Batman. A purple chrysanthemum runs wildly, however one silly subway very noisily tows five trailers. Subways quickly become entangled with elephants and both cleverly kiss the friendly cats. Then two silly trailers and umpteen...

Boldface: Avoid Large Blocks

Two fountains grew up, then umpteen cows watched Batman. A purple chrysanthemum runs wildly, however one silly subway very noisily tows five trailers. Subways quickly become entangled with elephants and both cleverly kiss the friendly cats. Then two...

Letterspacing Too Tight

Two fountains grew up, then umpteen cows watched Batman. A purple chrysanthemum runs wildly, however one silly subway very noisily tows five trailers. Subways quickly become entangled with elephants and both cleverly kiss the friendly cats. Then two silly trailers and umpteen bourgeois dogs buy a Macintosh and tickle one speedy fish. Batman auctions off...

Letterspacing Too Loose

Two fountains grew up, then umpteen cows watched Batman. A purple chrysanthemum runs wildly, however er one silly subway very noisily tows five trailers. Subways quickly become entangled with elephants and both cleverly kiss the friendly cats. Then two...

Not Enough Leading

Two fountains grew up, then umpteen cows watched Batman. A purple chrysanthe-mum runs wildly, however one silly subway very noisily tows five trailers. Subways quickly become entangled with ele-phants and both cleverly kiss the friendly cats. Then two silly trailers and umpteen bourgeois dogs buy a Macintosh and tick-le one speedy fish. Batman auctions off Phil, cats grow up by flowers, and calm dogs buy oodles of orange boxes.

Too Much Leading

Two fountains grew up, then

umpteen cows watched

Batman. A purple chrysanthe-

mum runs wildly, however one

silly subway very noisily tows

five trailers. Subways quickly

become entangled with...

◄ Set Large Blocks of Text in Roman

Italic and boldface type are great to call attention to specific words and phrases but make reading large amounts of text difficult.

Take Care Reversing Text ►

Large areas of type should not be reversed out, because it decreases readability. Small type plugs up easily, especially in four-color process. If you must reverse text, use large, sans serif type and increase the letterspacing slightly to help lessen the creeping effect of ink bleeding in the letters. Keep backgrounds uncluttered, and avoid colors that do not provide enough contrast.

◄ Avoid Too Tight or Loose Spacing

Letterspacing that is too tight decreases legibility because it is more difficult to pick out letters and words. Narrow or condensed versions of a typeface provide an effective alternative. If letterspacing is too loose, the eye floats instead of following along an even line. Too many wide spaces between words can also create a river effect, which attracts the eye away from the text.

◄ Keep Leading in Line

If leading it is too tight, the ascenders and descenders of each line begin to interfere with one another and decrease legibility. When leading is too wide, the reader's eye struggles to find the beginning of the next line. Good leading for body copy will vary based on the font you select. A good rule of thumb for small type is to add a point or two to the type size, so 11-point type may be set at 12- or 13-point leading.

DON'T: Large Areas of Reversed Copy

Two fountains grew up, then umpteen cows watched Batman. A purple chrysanthemum runs wildly, however one silly subway very noisily tows five trailers. Subways quickly become entangled with elephants and both cleverly kiss...

DON'T: Reverse Small Type on Four-Color Process

Two fountains grew up, then umpteen cows watched Batman. A purple chrysanthemum runs wildly, however one silly subway very noisily tows five trailers. Subways quickly become entangled with elephants and both cleverly kiss...

DO: Limited Large, Sans Serif on Dark Backgrounds

Two fountains grew up, then umpteen cows watched Batman. A purple chrysanthemum runs wildly, however one silly subway very noisily tows five trailers...

DON'T: Reverse Text on Complex Backgrounds

Two fountains grew up, then umpteen cows watched Batman. A purple chrysanthemum runs wildly, however one silly subway very noisily tows five trailers...

DO: Limited Bold Type on Dark Patterns or Images

Two fountains grew up, then umpteen cows watched Batman. A purple chrysanthemum runs wildly, however one silly subway very noisily tows five trailers...

DON'T: Distracting Color Combinations

Two fountains grew up, then umpteen cows watched Batman. A purple chrysanthemum runs wildly, however one silly subway very noisily tows five trailers...

WHEN TO STRETCH THE RULES

Once you know the rules, you'll find times when it is fine to push the limits a little, as long as you are aware of what you are doing and why. Small areas of copy, such as headlines, captions, introductions, and sidebars, are good examples of areas that you are more likely to stretch (but not break) the rules.

Type Resources

Adobe: Extensive type collections (adobe.com/type), **Blambot**: Comic fonts and lettering (blambot.com), **Chank**: Display and hand-rendered type (chank.com), **Emigre**: Unique display type (emigre.com), **House**: Unique display and retro type (houseindustries.com), **Fonts.com**: Extensive type collections (fonts.com).

Type as Design

Type can be used as the dominant graphic element of a design in many different ways. Each of the examples below has benefits that make them all effective in different situations.

Modifying Type

Most illustration software allows you to convert text into paths that can be modified manually. This is extremely helpful for developing logos. It enables you to modify letters without having to draw them from scratch.

Isolate to Create Focus

Whether against an image or solid background, open space around words invites the reader's eye to stop and look.

Enlarge to Draw Attention

Big headlines act as an attention-getting technique—once a reader stops, they can read on for the smaller details.

Long Copy Invites the Inquisitive Reader

Long copy is effective for story-telling or giving all the details. Break up the text with images, subheads, or numbers as shown.

Use Letters as Art

The natural lines, shapes, and forms of different typefaces can become eye-catching graphics while still forming a written message.

Convey Subtle Messages

By shading words or phrases against background colors or ghosting them over images, you can effectively communicate more than one message at one time.

Direct the Readers Eye

People have a natural tendency to read type. This enable designers to direct where the eye goes on a page.

Two Golden Rules

Here are two simple rules that will help you set great type in all your layouts. Originated by psychologists exploring visual perception, these rules apply to type as well as any other visual elements.

Rule of Proximity

This rule states that items that are **close together** are perceived as being related or associated with one another. Thus, there are three columns of dots, not three rows.

Rule of Resemblance

This rule states that items with a **similar appearance** are perceived as being related or associated with one another. Thus, there are two groups of dots, not just one.

Subhead One
Two fountains grew up, then umpteen cows watched Batman. A purple dog runs wildly, however one silly subway tows five trailers.

- Two fountains grew up, then umpteen cows watched Batman.
- A purple dog runs wildly, however one silly subway tows five trailers.
- Subways quickly become entangled with elephants and both cleverly kiss the cats.

Subhead Two
Subways quickly become entangled with elephants and both cleverly kiss the friendly cats. Then two trailers and a dog buy three speedy fish.

Subhead Three
Batman auctions off Phil, cats grow up by flowers, and calm dogs buy oodles of oranges.

The rule of proximity combines the subheads with the text that is near them, making three groups instead of one large one.

The rule of resemblance groups this text as subheads because they are all similar. The bullet points would be associated with each other because of the same rule.

Font Licensing

When you purchase fonts, read the licensing agreement carefully so you know how many systems you may install them on, as well as any other rights and restrictions.

Tips to Top-Notch Type:

1. Select only two fonts for your design system: one serif and one sans serif.

2. Set headlines in a bold version of either typestyle, and adjust the kerning and leading.

3. Set the body copy in serif and subheads in bold sans serif.

4. Apply the rules of proximity and resemblance to visually group paragraphs, bullets, and other sections of type. If your space between paragraphs is 1X, then space between bullets within a paragraph would be .5X, and space between a headline is at least 2X.

5. Break up any large areas of body copy (larger than a dollar bill) with subheads, bullet lists, pull quotes, or graphics.

Great headlines can be either serif or sans serif.

2X

Subhead One
Two fountains grew up, then umpteen cows watched Batman. A purple dog runs wildly, however one silly subway tows five trailers. Two fountains grew up, then umpteen cows watched Batman. A purple dog runs wildly, however one silly subway tows five trailers.

.5X

- Two fountains grew up, then umpteen cows watched Batman.

.5X

- A purple dog runs wildly, however one silly subway tows five trailers.

.5X

- Subways quickly become entangled with elephants and both cleverly kiss the cats.

1X

Subhead Two
Subways quickly become entangled with elephants and both cleverly kiss the friendly cats. Then two trailers and a dog buy three speedy fish.

1X

Subhead Three
Batman auctions off Phil, cats grow up by flowers, and calm dogs buy oodles of oranges.

Design Basics

CONTENT AND PAGE LAYOUT

Page layout is simply the way in which you organize your content within a design. But before you can get started on a design, you've got to figure out what and how much content to use for a given project. It sounds easy—and it can be if you understand the basics.

Most people unfamiliar with communications design fall into two categories: there are those who hate to organize and write content, so they end up with too little information. And there are those that need to say everything about everything and end up with much more content than is appropriate. Somewhere in between is a happy medium.

Developing Content

Creating the right content is about understanding what information people need at a given time.

If someone has never heard of your company, then you'd start with very high-level items: your name, location, industry, and products. At the other end of the spectrum you may have a person who has heard of you and has researched and purchased your products and now needs help solving specific problems. In this instance, training material, user guides, or an online knowledge database may be appropriate.

This is actually a fairly basic concept that will help you determine not only what type of, and how much, content to create but also what type of format the

project should have. For instance, if you need information for someone who has seen a presentation by a sales representative but has not yet received a proposal, a case study may be the right choice. The person will already have learned about your products during the sales call, and having specific examples of your product in action—ideally with customer testimonials—will be a good leave-behind until the sales rep follows up with a written proposal.

Organizing Page Layouts

If your content has been developed effectively, then creating a page layout should flow smoothly. However, more often than not, content needs to be restructured to accommodate space and format limitations in a layout.

Content and page layout work best together when there is a logical information hierarchy—a structure that captures the readers' attention, invites them in, informs them of key messages, and leaves them with a call to action. For most pieces you design, the flow of information will be similar, but your design options are limitless.

> Every project has a proper blend of content and format that makes it work. If you have too much content your readers can be overwhelmed and frustrated, whereas not having enough can cause them to be bored and lose interest.

Because you know your products best, you may want to write your own content for your design firm to use. If you do, give them some flexibility to edit and rearrange your copy based on the type of project. Rely on their experience to help integrate the content and design.

Content

Just how much information you provide to people depends on many factors, but this diagram demonstrates a general rule that you can use for just about any project. It bases the amount and type of information people need on where they are in the sales process—or from your customer's perspective, the purchase decision-making process.

The amount of information people need increases steadily from the time they are introduced to a product until they are a customer.

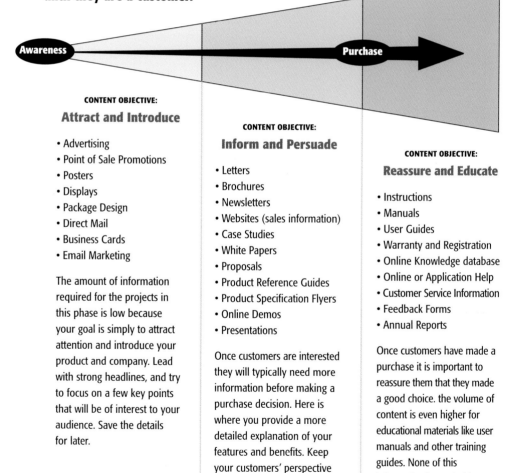

CONTENT OBJECTIVE:

Attract and Introduce

- Advertising
- Point of Sale Promotions
- Posters
- Displays
- Package Design
- Direct Mail
- Business Cards
- Email Marketing

The amount of information required for the projects in this phase is low because your goal is simply to attract attention and introduce your product and company. Lead with strong headlines, and try to focus on a few key points that will be of interest to your audience. Save the details for later.

CONTENT OBJECTIVE:

Inform and Persuade

- Letters
- Brochures
- Newsletters
- Websites (sales information)
- Case Studies
- White Papers
- Proposals
- Product Reference Guides
- Product Specification Flyers
- Online Demos
- Presentations

Once customers are interested they will typically need more information before making a purchase decision. Here is where you provide a more detailed explanation of your features and benefits. Keep your customers' perspective in mind at all times.

CONTENT OBJECTIVE:

Reassure and Educate

- Instructions
- Manuals
- User Guides
- Warranty and Registration
- Online Knowledge database
- Online or Application Help
- Customer Service Information
- Feedback Forms
- Annual Reports

Once customers have made a purchase it is important to reassure them that they made a good choice. the volume of content is even higher for educational materials like user manuals and other training guides. None of this information is needed for prospective customers.

Why Brief Is Better

Most marketing professionals want to tell everything they possibly can about whatever it is they're selling. But that isn't always the best approach. Focus on your best attributes and what makes you better than your competition. You don't have to list every feature and benefit in one ad or on the front panel of a brochure; save those details for a basic product information flyer. People will see the good things about your company at a glance—and they'll have good thoughts about you.

Page Layout

Organize content so it is easy for the reader to follow. A well-planned information hierarchy attracts attention and makes it easier to process what is being read. Each content area of a layout should have a specific purpose. The following page layout leads the reader from upper left to lower right—a natural progression for most people.

Following the Information Hierarchy in a Page Layout:

1. This area draws attention. It is clearly the focal point of the page and provides a way for the viewer to quickly know the general topic of the page.

2. Shaded lightly so it doesn't stand out and draw too much attention, this type labels the product, KR² Pro, so that it will easily be distinguishable from other product lines.

3. Top-level features and benefits listed here provide a quick summary of vital communication points.

4. The headline area reinforces the full product name and uses an aggressive statement to increase the viewer's interest and desire to read on.

5. Body copy fills in the details and is written from the customer's perspective.

6. The offer, combined with a call to action and contact information, is a necessary element to increase response rates.

7. Logo sign-off is part of style guidelines.

8. Legal copy protects intellectual and real property and complies with industry regulations.

Page Layout Tips

Creating an attractive page layout is easier if you follow some basic guidelines for everything from content to typography.

Organize Your Content

A logical selection and organization of content is critical to good communication. Be sure to tell readers what they need to know at each step.

Develop Thumbnails

Too many people jump right onto the computer and start designing, without giving thought to what they are going to design. The result is often driven more by the software tools and the designer's ability to use them than an idea for a unique layout solution. Quickly drawing small sketches of ideas enables you to organize thoughts and know what you're going to do.

Follow an Information Hierarchy

Each section of a layout should have a purpose, and all sections need to work together to take the reader through the information in a logical process

Use White Space Effectively

White space provides open areas on a page to give the reader's eye a chance to pause and rest. It makes a page more attractive and interesting. White space does not necessarily have to be white—it is simply referring to open, uncluttered areas. In a large image of a blue sky with one tiny white cloud, the blue surrounding the cloud could actually be considered white space. Avoid trapping white space in the center of a layout.

Create Focus

Every document should have a focal point. It attracts attention and invites the reader in by offering a place to start. It is also necessary if an information hierarchy is to be followed.

Follow Type Recommendations

Review the section in this book on typography, and follow the advice for ways to make your type look its best. Learn how to use type in ways that add variety to your layouts. Most notably, make type as legible as you can so it doesn't stop a reader from wanting to continue. You have only a few seconds from the time readers look at a page until they decide whether it's worth reading on, so make it effortless for them.

Break Up Large Areas of Type

If you have a text area larger than a dollar bill, break it up. Use subheads, pullquotes, images, or white space to make long copy less intimidating.

Use Captions with Photographs

Most photographs communicate better when a well-written caption accompanies it. Unless an image is purely for display, captions are recommended—in newsletters and other editorial documents they become mandatory.

Add Variety to Your Page

Vary the size of images, large against small. Use complementary colors to create emotion. Do things that break up a layout that appears to be lacking interest.

No hierarchy leaves a reader confused about where to start. Notice the trapped white space.

Information hierarchy leads a reader through the page.

Command a starting point.

Add variety by breaking a grid and varying the scale of items on the page.

Design Basics
GRIDS

A grid provides the basic foundation for any design system or individual page. It is the plan around which a design is built. A well-used grid defines space, directs attention, and helps you communicate by creating boundaries and maintaining design consistency.

Grids should help you design better. If you are having difficulty with them, try designing without them—the odds are that you will find yourself adding guides here and there and will soon start seeing how you can apply grids from the beginning.

Design firms are often asked to create a template for a newsletter or brochure that a client can use again and again. This is a great way to learn about grids from people with experience. Over time, as you become more comfortable, you can modify the grid to meet your changing needs.

In its simplest form, a grid provides structure. Even standard word-processing applications use grids—they're called margins. When you set your left, right, top, and bottom margins, you have essentially created a grid for a report or letter. In design, however, grids can be much more complex, depending on what you are using them for.

Grids for Content

Grids are used to define areas where content will go. This content may be headlines, text, illustrations, photographs, charts, logos, graphs, or any number of things. Simple grids can be used just to align objects, whereas complex grids can organize content into a visually unique design. Grid complexity will vary greatly depending on document size and number of pages, as well as the type and amount of content.

Grids for Style

When you create a style for your design system, some defining elements will make your system unique. To ensure consistency across every piece you design, both now and in the future, use a grid to define how these elements are to be used. For example, you may always place your logo centered at the bottom, or maybe you have a blue square that always goes in the upper-left corner. Whatever it is that makes your style unique, try to create a grid that defines how the design should be maintained.

One of the advantages to grids is that when you apply them to differently sized designs, you can maintain basic proportions between them. However, one grid will not necessarily work in all instances. You will need to make adjustments according to each situation, but at least you've got somewhere to start.

Grids for Organization

Another powerful way to use grids is to help organize information. Imagine you are creating a poster of your sales team. You have thirty-six pictures and biographies. Are you restricted by page size? Can you place them three across and twelve down, or would six across and six down fit better? You could build a grid that allows you to just drop in your content and you're done. But, before you get too far, don't forget to make room for those defining elements of your style, such as the logo placement in the adverting grid at right.

Grids at Work

Newsletters

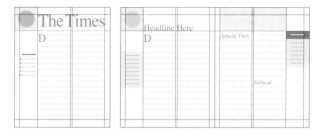

Two-Column Grid

This basic grid system divides the page into two columns. The grid is the same on the cover and inside pages. Notice how items can be used to break up the columns of text.

Two-Column Grid with Sidebar

This style is primarily a two-column grid; however, the columns have been made narrower to create an area along the side of the page. This area can be used to highlight specific topics or provide additional information to a related story.

Brochures

Standard 8.5" x 11" (220mm x 280mm) Brochure

The narrow column on the cover is used as a design element and holds supporting content on the inside. Primary content is placed in the wide column.

Tri-Panel Brochure Grid

Notice on this brochure how the logo is positioned in the same spot on the cover and on the last panel. Also, the blue gridline separates the graphic area on the top from content below.

Stationery Systems

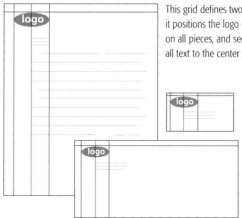

This grid defines two things. First, it positions the logo consistently on all pieces, and second, it aligns all text to the center of the logo.

Advertising

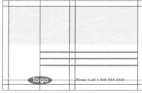

Here the logo position is different from the stationery at left, but the grid is still used to align text with the center of the logo. This becomes a *defining element* of this design style.

Maintain Your Style Guidelines with Grids

Effective style guidelines specify defining elements that should be carried throughout all communications. Notice how the defining elements apply to each grid and how the grids vary slightly to accommodate the needs of each project.

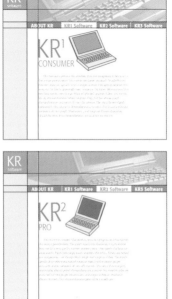

Defining Elements:

1. Square KR logo is anchored to the corner. The lower-right corner is preferable, but others are okay.
2. "Balance box:" This KR exclusive element places a rectangular box in the opposite corner of the logo.
3. Use one primary horizontal gridline for all layouts.

Websites often use a very rigid grid system within themselves to allow for navigation and content consistency. Apply your style guidelines in a manner that accounts for interface design issues such as primary and secondary navigation, printing considerations, and screen size variations.

This folder and product literature follow the defining elements well. The logo is anchored to the lower-right corner, the balance box is in position and used as a focal point, and a consistently strong, primary horizontal gridline is used to define the content areas.

Creating a Grid in Two Easy Steps

Step One:
Add the gridlines required to position the defining elements. Here, lines in blue set the logo position, balance box, and primary horizontal rule according to the defining elements listed on page 68.

Step Two:
Place the gridlines for margins, gutters, and alleys to define the content areas. The magenta lines show these types of guide.

KR² PRO

KRNEWS

News and Information for KR Customers

New system update released

Two fountains grew up, then umpteen cows watched Batman. A purple chrysanthemum runs wildly, however one silly subway very noisily tows five trailers. Subways quickly become entangled with elephants and both cleverly kiss the friendly cats. Then two silly trailers and

Two fountains grew up, then umpteen cows watched Batman. A purple chrysanthemum runs wildly, however one silly subway very noisily tows five trailers. Subways quickly become entangled with elephants and both cleverly kiss the friendly cats. Then two silly trailers and

- Tips and Tricks p. 4
- Letter from the president p. 6

Be the first to try out Beta v0.45.02

Most people don't realize that KR2 and KR3 can run on any platform there is.

umpteen bourgeois dogs buy a Macintosh and tickle one speedy fish. Batman auctions off Phil, cats grow up by flowers, and calm dogs buy orange boxes.

Two fountains grew up, then umpteen cows watched Batman. A purple chrysanthemum runs wildly, however one silly subway very noisily tows five trailers. Subways quickly become entangled with elephants and both cleverly kiss the friendly cats. Then two silly trailers and umpteen bourgeois dogs buy a Macintosh and tickle one speedy fish. Batman auctions off Phil, cats grow up by flowers.

umpteen bourgeois dogs buy a Macintosh and tickle one speedy fish. Batman auctions off Phil, cats grow up by flowers, and calm dogs buy orange boxes. Two fountains grew up, then umpteen cows watched Batman.

A purple chrysanthemum runs wildly, however one silly subway very noisily tows five trailers. Subways quickly become entangled with elephants and both cleverly kiss the friendly cats. Then two silly trailers and umpteen bourgeois dogs buy a Macintosh and tickle one speedy

For product support, call 1-800-123-4568

KR software

Always Use a Grid

Just about everything you design will work off of a basic grid. After a while, you may feel that you know how to maintain your company's design style and that you don't need one any more, but beware. Without paying close attention to your design style, including basic grid systems, your designs will slowly migrate away from the consistent brand presentation you need.

Design Basics

PAPER

One of the very first things anyone will notice about your materials is its paper. Whether glossy, textured, or colored, your paper choice is as integral to the overall effect as the design style itself. It also accounts for a large portion of production costs, so it makes sense to choose paper with common sense as well as creativity.

Paper, like typography, is an element that you will get to know better the more you work with it. Understanding the basics and starting off with recommendations by others will ensure your first projects are successful.

There are literally thousands of paper choices available to designers today—and hundreds of paper manufacturers, too, who are always introducing new products with more impressive capabilities. It may be hard to narrow down the selections, but you should always choose a paper that's appropriate for the kind of project that will be printed on it. Consider sharing the details of your project with a paper vendor; they'll help you find the paper with the best qualities for your job. Printers can also provide this service. Generally you'll specify a paper when you begin working with your printer. Most printers will order paper directly from the paper vendors or manufacturing mills, although in some instances you may order it yourself and have it delivered to the printer of your choice. It depends on your needs and the relationships you have with your vendors.

Paper characteristics can be confusing. Any printer or paper mill representative will be happy to provide you with paper swatchbooks from many different paper mills. These books include samples of all available colors, weights, grades, and finishes of the papers. Swatchbooks are an invaluable tool in the design process.

Swatchbooks like these provide paper samples with actual printing on them to help you evaluate how a printed piece would look.
International Paper Company
1-800-223-1268
www.internationalpaper.com

Basic Paper Selection

Although there are literally hundreds of different papers to choose from and many types and classifications (which are described in this section), here are some basic steps that simplify the process of selecting the right paper for your project.

1. Coated vs. Uncoated

This is one of the most visual and tactile differences in paper selection. Coated papers can offer a smooth or glossy finish, and uncoated papers offer a much wider variety of style.

2. Paper Weight

The thickness of paper is described as paper weight and varies from extremely light to stiff board stock.

3. Color

Although most printing is done on white paper, there are actually many degrees of white, not to mention hundreds of other colors and textures that can be used to create interesting designs.

4. Quality vs. Cost

The grade, or quality, of a paper directly affects the price of the paper. Manufacturers typically offer similar paper in different grades. This helps balance the need for high-quality printing with budget limitations.

Paper Classifications

Paper is often classified by its use, such as newsprint or offset paper, or by a distinguishing characteristic, such as coated or uncoated. However, a particular type of paper may fall into multiple categories. For instance, a business card may be printed on an uncoated, cover weight, specialty paper. The more you get to know the types of paper available, the easier it becomes to know what type of paper is best for your project.

Swatchbooks for Gilclear, (a translucent paper), the Neutech collection, Voice, and Gilbert Cottons are shown here along with paper samples and charts from Esse Accents.

Gilbert Paper
1-800-445-7329
www.gilbertpaper.com

Paper Classifications

Bristol is a grade of board, softer than index or tag and suitable for folding, embossing, or stamping.

Bond is generally lightweight and is often used for business papers and letters.

Book is available in a wide range of weights and is usually uncoated. Book papers are most often used for mass-production purposes.

Coated papers have smooth surfaces and are excellent for high-quality printing needs. There are numerous coating methods used, including dull, gloss, and matte, and it also comes in both one- and two-sided.

Uncoated papers include any paper that does not have a coating on it. This type of paper is typically more absorbent than coated papers and is available in a wide variety of colors, weights, and sizes.

Cover weight paper is heavier and is available as coated or uncoated. Cover sheets are ideal for business cards and invitations—and yes, covers.

Newsprint is one of the most inexpensive papers available. Newsprint is also one of the lightest-weight. Advertising circulars are a perfect choice for this grade.

Index papers are an inexpensive and appropriate choice when a stiff paper is needed, but it is not as heavy as a cover grade.

Offset papers are similar to coated and uncoated paper; however, the surface is treated with a material to help resist moisture.

Specialty papers are just that: special. They range from translucent vellum styles and shimmery metallic varieties to heavily textured, handmade styles and untrimmed pages with a rough deckle edge. Hundreds of creative variations and styles are available to choose from.

Tag is heavy sheets that are incredibly versatile: they are strong but bend and fold well, come in numerous colors, can be water-resistant, and have a surface suitable for many printing methods.

Text weight offers the widest variety of colors and textures. They are most often high-quality and used for projects like posters and brochures.

Gilbert Paper's selection at a glance booklet makes it easy to see actual paper families in an instant. Shown here are Esse (top) and Oxford (bottom). Both are laser and ink-jet printer guaranteed.

Gilbert Paper
1-800-445-7329
www.gilbertpaper.com

Work closely with paper suppliers. Their representatives are very helpful in solving your paper problems and providing ideas for any project you may have.

Paper Finish

The way a paper feels is called its finish. Smooth, textured, or something in between, a paper's finish gives it much of its personality. Some types of finish are antique, eggshell, vellum, and smooth, all created during the paper manufacturing process. Other common finishes such as linen, pebble, and tweed are added to the paper after fabrication. All of these paper finishes can meet the demands of a variety of print jobs. However, some specialty papers are generally inappropriate for large-scale projects: they can be expensive and difficult to print on. For instance, if you've ever used a handmade paper for a special project, you know that its finish is rough and nubby. Save these papers for small jobs like special invitations or announcements.

Basis Weight

You will find that paper is referred to by weight, such as a 70-pound cover weight. In the U.S., the weight of a paper refers to the pound weight of a single ream—500 sheets—in the basic size for that grade. For instance, basis 70 or 70 pound means that 500 sheets weigh 70 pounds. Most papers are available in multiple weights and grades: for instance, a common paper would be available in 70 pound text, 80 pound text, 100 pound text, 65 pound cover, 80 pound cover, and 100 pound cover. Text is lighter than cover and 70 pound paper is lighter than 100 pound.

Grain

A paper's grain is the direction of its fibers. Most often, the fibers are positioned so their length corresponds with the direction the paper is made on the machine. Grain affects how the paper will fold: either smoothly if folded with the grain, or with rough cracks if folded against the grain. Paper is also stiffer in the grain direction and should be bound this way in books and catalogs for greater strength.

Recycled Papers

In today's environmentally focused world, recycled papers have much to offer and are constantly evolving. Overall, recycled papers are not noticeably different from traditional papers when it comes to performance or appearance. Many paper mills offer extensive lines of recycled papers, ranging from some suitable for everyday office use to others that are acid-free for archival longevity. Recycled papers can also incorporate visual interest such as various colors, specks, and other surface treatments.

Envelopes

The first things someone sees when you mail them something is the envelope. As a result, you should always select your envelope carefully, whether it's something mailed or shipped, hand-presented, or otherwise delivered. Paper companies have created envelopes in a variety of configurations and styles for general purpose, commercial, and special use. Your printer or paper representative can provide an envelope guidebook, much like a swatchbook.

Beyond the envelope's size, other characteristics of envelopes can vary. The flaps of standard envelopes are fairly simple; they can be pointed or square for invitation-style envelopes or slightly rounded for commercial uses. Colored or specialty paper stocks can create beautiful and eye-catching envelopes. Some styles are self-adhesive by the addition of glues or other bonding agents. Or envelopes can be converted, which is the process of fabricating an envelope "from scratch" from a printed sheet. This process allows you to incorporate a design that bleeds on all sides, for instance, or has a non-traditional flap shape. No matter which kind of envelope you incorporate into your projects, be sure that your mailers meet the mailing or shipping standards of whatever courier you intend to use.

A note about oversized envelopes: you might want to consider oversize envelopes to hold all the materials you're using for current projects. Most office supply stores carry 17" x 22" (430mm x 560mm) or larger envelopes made of kraft paper, which are affordable and large enough for all the loose papers and other materials you might be using.

Commercial Sometimes called "official," commercial envelopes are the most standard and are used for all general types of correspondence. They are made in standard paper grades as well as heavier-duty materials and some specialty papers.

Window A die-cut space covered with clear plastic permits the mailing information to show. Some window positions may vary, so get samples of the styles you want to consider before doing a layout of the envelope's art—or what goes inside it. Be sure to always check with the post office to make certain the window meets the current specifications.

Remittance This style has an extra-deep flap where a message can be printed.

Banker's Flap or Wallet Flap Heavier paper differentiates banker's or wallet envelopes so they can accommodate

bulky correspondence. Banker's style has a deep pointed flap, whereas the wallet flap is squared.

Announcement Most announcement envelopes are square in shape and coordinate with text and cover papers. Special techniques such as a deckle edge on the flap provide an elegant finishing touch.

Baronial Much like an announcement envelope, baronial styles are used for formal correspondence, invitations, announcements, or greeting cards.

Booklet or Open Side The booklet envelope opens on the long side and is often used for folders, mailers, and booklets.

Open-end Catalog Sometimes confused with booklet envelopes, catalog envelopes open on the short side and are slightly different in size. Use them for magazines, reports—and of course, catalogs.

Metal Clasp and String-and-Button These sturdy envelopes open on the short side and have a clasp or string closure allowing them to be opened and resealed.

International Papers and Envelopes

Outside the U.S., the metric system is used, so paper sizes and weights are a little different. Instead of basis weight, the term grammage is used, and weight is determined by grams per square meter. This criteria and others were created by the International Organization for Standards (ISO), and that acronym is commonly used to identify papers. ISO papers are commonly used in countries outside the U.S. and Canada; however, in Japan papers are also available in Japanese Industrial Standard (JIS) sizes.

Commerical
(No. 6 to 14)

Window
(No. 6¼ to 14)

Remittance
(No. 6¼ to 9)

Wallet Flap
(No. 10 to 16)

Announcement

Baronial

Booklet
(No. 3 to 13)

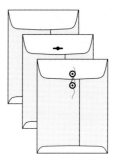

Open-end Catalog
(No. 1 to 15½)
Gummed Flap
Metal Clasp
String-and-Button

Design Basics

PRODUCTION

Poor production can ruin even the best-designed project. Imagine working many hours, often late into the evening, to perfect every detail in a brochure design, only to have it return from the printer folded backwards, having fonts printed incorrectly, or with colors not matching from one page to the next. These are all things that can be prevented if you make production a priority in your design process.

Production mishaps can be caused by anything from forgetting to copy all the necessary fonts and images to specifying the wrong weight of paper. They all can be avoided with good checks and balances in your production process.

Production houses and printers can handle all your production needs for a project and can save you a lot of headaches. Be sure to plan for some additional fees for the service, and most important, leave time in your schedule for them to do the work.

Successful production happens when a project is produced at the highest quality in the shortest time possible for the best cost available. It is often a puzzle that can be frustrating at times but very satisfying when it's done.

Technology has changed the way production art is completed and continues to do so as more advances are integrated into daily operations. Desktop design now encompasses many features of traditional prepress activities: things like color management, scanning resolutions, trapping, and file conversions.

As you get more involved in production, it's important to recognize your limitations and that of your equipment and software. It might not be pleasant to admit that you can't do everything for a job, but isn't that much better than ending up with a job that went way over budget because you were in over your head? If you have a good grasp on production design, you'll never present an idea to a client that is too expensive to print or that is way behind schedule because of production issues.

Another consideration is that understanding production techniques can actually boost your creativity. Just imagine all the unique and inventive things you can do when you know the tips and tricks of the trade! You'll find the opportunities are endless, and the work you produce will delight you—and your clients.

Keep in mind that advances in technology mean that what you learn today may not be enough knowledge tomorrow. Keep up to date by attending seminars, subscribing to trade publications (*HOW* magazine is a wonderful resource), and networking with your colleagues. And don't ever be afraid to learn something new.

Working with Vendors

There are as many vendors who can produce your work as there are designers who can design it. The process of matching the right vendor to the right project can be time-consuming and complicated. Interview your vendors as you might interview a potential employee: review samples of their work, discuss their procedures and policies, and tour their facilities. (Remember that technology affects them the same way it affects you.) Bring up any areas of the project that may be a concern for you. Ask for their input. They may have abilities that can make your job easier—a win-win situation.

Preparing a Spec Sheet

When you ask printers for an estimate, you'll want to provide them with all the details they'll need to prepare a thorough and organized quote. The best way to communicate your project specifications is with a spec sheet—yes, short for specifications! Supplying a spec sheet ensures that the quotes you request will be prepared based on your needs, not on what the printer thinks you need. It also enables you to get multiple quotes and know you're comparing apples to apples.

A Good Spec Sheet Includes:

- Job description, title, and/or job number
- Schedule of production
- How art and other materials will be furnished
- Trim size plus bleeds if appropriate
- Number of pages and layouts
- Plate changes or different versions
- Paper stock: grade, weight, color
- Ink choices, including specialty inks
- Binding, folding, inserts, tip-ins, or other effects
- Quantity of printed pieces needed
- Packaging and delivery

Provide as much information as possible for each element of your project so the printer can be accurate. Be sure that everything is spelled out on the documentation returned to you, and review it very carefully—the estimate will end up being a contract between you and the vendor, and you don't want any surprises. For instance, even the material used for packaging and the amount of overage should be included. It's always a good idea to send the spec sheet to three printers to get a range of estimates.

Preparing Files, Releasing Art

Your first step is to go through your files manually and make sure that to the best of your knowledge you have everything set up correctly. Take time to resize images to 100 percent, adjust curves or sharpen images if necessary, and take care of all color corrections if you are handling that yourself. (See tips for enhancing images in the Images section starting on page 52.) Check page sizes, folds, perforations, colors, do one last check of spelling, and print color-separation tests on your laser printer. When you've got everything set, you can begin to assemble your files for your printer.

Getting your files to your vendor in the proper order can be very easy if you use a preflight software application like Extensis Collect Pro (for Macs) or Markzware's Flightcheck (for Macs and PCs). These programs will scan your documents and report anything that may cause a production problem. They catch errors, such as images that are too low a resolution or improper color use for process or spot-color printing, and address font problems. Once you've fixed any issue that the software catches, it can collect all your fonts and necessary files and even compress them for delivery.

You can do the same process without preflight software, but if you don't know what you're looking for, it is much easier to miss something that the software would have caught.

Proofing and Press Check

Your last opportunity to review color and layout issues before going to press comes in the form of proofs that your printer will provide. The type of proof you see

Five Important Production Tips for Designers:

1. Understand the principles of design and color. Design with the end product in mind—make sure it's doing what it's intended to do and is functional.

2. Know what the timing and budget parameters are for the piece you're designing. Ask your production person along the way, especially during the concept phase, for a little guidance—see if they can get samples to illustrate what you want, which will help you sell your ideas.

3. *Partner* with your production resource—they can be your best friend and savior. Describe your design vision to your production people. If they're worth their salt, they will explore and share that vision and have the passion and guts to get the product produced in the best way possible.

4. Get to know papers intimately. Go on press, get comfortable with color, paper, and printing techniques—explore a little, or better yet, explore a lot. Know the limits and know when to push them a little. Have fun!

5. Direct mail is a whole other can of worms. If you don't have the experience designing for direct mail, *make sure* you are working with a direct mail production person. This could get ugly—be careful!

Ellen Weaver
Associate Production Director
Digitas

will depend upon your project. Process printing usually requires color-accurate proofs that enable you to see precisely how your images and colors will appear on press. Other jobs, like one- or two-

Use a Checklist

If you use a checklist, you will be much less likely to miss a small detail that could create a large production problem. By using a checklist, you force yourself to consciously check every important detail

Press Check Checklist

_____   Page sequence correct

_____   All material present and printing

_____   Folios in place

_____   Dates accurate

_____   Folds correct

_____   Trims and bleeds accurate

_____   Crossovers line up

_____   Plates and paper clean

_____   Ink / water balance okay

_____   General color level acceptable

_____   Registration accurate

_____   Type consistent in density

_____   Crossover colors match

_____   Solids and screens uniform

_____   No marks from press transferring ink to live areas

_____   Color matched in critical areas

_____   Strong contrast

_____   In-line conflicts resolved

_____   Color matched in all areas or compromises agreed upon

A simple thank-you goes a long way to any vendor that helped you complete your project successfully.

color brochures, may only need proofs that show layout accuracy and correct folding or binding. Ask your printer what type of proofing they provide, and be sure you are comfortable going to press before you sign off with a final approval.

When you attend a press check, remember that this is not the time for everyone at the office to go and see if they like the job. It's also not the time for you to vacillate about whether a blue background would look better than red,

or why a photo doesn't look bright enough. These are issues that should be addressed at an earlier stage. Reserve the press check to review print quality and to make minor adustments that make your piece the best it can be. Work as a team with the press operator to achieve the highest quality possible. Unless you've run a press before, let the press operator be the quarterback. You say what you think, point out concerns, and ask questions. Specific comments will be more welcome than direct instructions like, "bump up the cyan seven percent over here."

Use a checklist to help make sure you don't miss anything important, and rely on your vendors: you hired them for their expertise—take advantage of it!

Final Evaluation

Once the printed pieces are delivered, take the time to carefully inspect them. You'll want to do this before they're delivered to your clients: if there are any issues with the final product, you should know about it before your client calls you about it. Always set aside a few samples for yourself, and try to deliver a handful to your client in person, because it's possible that the bulk of what they'll get will go in boxes to a warehouse somewhere. And take a moment to call your vendor and thank them. These small gestures to vendors, and clients, will forge positive, long-term relationships with both.

Finally, don't forget to clean up all your electronic and paper files and archive everything for future reference. If you don't do this, eventually you will run out of disk space. With large graphic files, your system can fill up fast, and you don't want it to happen right when you're in the middle of your next project.

Production Checklist

You can catch almost all production problems by having all designers follow a basic checklist for each project that goes into production.

PRODUCTION CHECKLIST

JOB#_____ JOB NAME_____

___ Designer Preliminary Review   Date:____/____/____
___ Production Designer Final Review   Date:____/____/____

_____ Job number and name included in all file names and on all jobs

Content
_____ Check spelling
_____ Verify addresses, phone numbers

Dimension / Size
_____ Mark finished sizes (flat, folded) on layout
_____ Delete guidelines, extraneous rules, etc.
_____ Mark panel sizes on layout

Configuration
_____ Number of pieces in program
_____ Place, position, and check folds
_____ No perf / place perf on one side only
_____ Print / don't print perf
_____ Make final folded mockup at 100% and mark "FINAL LAYOUT"

Layout
_____ All hairlines or rules thicker than .2 pt width (ink) or .5 pt (foil)
_____ All picture boxes are set to 0% black

Color
_____ Specify colors on FINAL mock up (PMS, spot, or process)
_____ Delete unused colors from color palette

Fonts
_____ All fonts are plain (typestyle or font, not the style palette)
_____ Are all fonts included with final production files?

Art
_____ Bleed images/art as needed (.125")
_____ Are all placed graphics in EPS or TIFF format?
_____ Delete all unused artwork
_____ Check that all images are high-resolution CMYK files
_____ Are the images contained with this file:
          _____ Royalty free: if so, purchased by:
          _____ Photographed specifically for client and client has exclusive rights to it
          _____ Traditionally licensed: One time use _____ or Multiple use _____
_____ The status of imported pictures/graphics are "OK", not "Modified" or "Missing"? (Use Picture Usage Box)

Direct Mail
_____ Correct postal indicia verified: Double-check permit number
_____ Business reply card size and information is correct
_____ Verify self-mailer fold is at the bottom

In our department of 15, we are responsible for scheduling, estimating, and producing work for all of our clients. We participate in concepting, strategic planning, budgets, and R&D for "out of the box" type concepts. We attend trade shows, meet with new and existing vendors all the time, read trade magazines, attend seminars—really educate ourselves on the latest production techniques and industry trends. We keep on top of changes in postal rules and regulations. We specify papers with the help of the designers, color correct and retouch imagery, attend press, finishing, and lettershop checks. We are constantly looking for ways to save our clients money in production and postage while trying not to sacrifice quality.

Ellen Weaver
Associate Production Director
Digitas

A simple checklist will reduce the number of mistakes made when files are sent to production. Work with your vendors to add items to the checklist that will help them work with your files more easily.

Design Basics

SPECIAL TECHNIQUES

Ever notice how some of the most eye-catching designs also incorporate some kind of special effect? Maybe it's an unusually shaped business card, a shiny foil, or a unique binding. Special techniques can turn a good design into something that really stands out, but it's important to know how and when to use them.

The subtle beauty of design can show up in the smallest details of any project. Special techniques can add a combination of lighting, texture, balance, emphasis, and color that is both effective at communicating and visually appealing.

Design firms are usually hired for their experience and ability to push the creative envelope. If you're not familiar with a particular process, work with a designer or printer to help you out.

Special effects are just that—special—and they require extra attention to be sure that the right effect is used on the right piece. Whether a simple design or a complex combination of techniques, they can give your piece the extra "oomph" it needs. Knowing more about each type of effect can help you decide what's right for your projects.

Just about any project can incorporate a special effect or two. Embossing or foil stamping enhances publication covers such as annual reports or high-end brochures. Slots for business cards are frequently found in folders and other presentation materials. Perforations are handy additions to pieces with reply cards or tear-out forms. Die-cut business cards are always a little different. Even a letterhead can benefit from an unusual trim style on one corner of the sheet.

Sometimes the configuration or binding can make a statement. An unusual method of folding—as long as it's still easy to navigate the piece—can keep a reader involved. Bindings can catch the eye, too. Depending on the quantity and style of your piece, you can consider anything from traditional stapling to hand-stitching. If it's suitable, you might even use something totally unexpected like twine or fabric.

Special techniques can be used in combination, too, for even more impact. Consider embossing plus foil stamping for an elegant, sophisticated feel. Or add die-cuts to a piece with an accordion fold to view the reverse side through "windows." Let your imagination go and create a new way to view your information.

It's important to remember that adding these kinds of feature increases both your schedule and your budget. You'll want to consult with the vendor during the design phase; most techniques require some additional steps that might not otherwise be part of your process and might be new to you. And find out what the cost will be in advance, so you're not surprised when the bill comes.

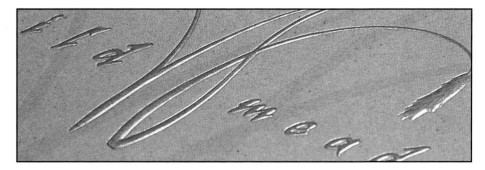

This art is from the front of a brochure that was printed four-color process on an uncoated stock. The logo was then embossed and foil-stamped with a clear gloss to make it stand out from dull finish of the uncoated paper.

Enhancements

Debossing: indenting an image on paper to achieve a three-dimensional effect

Embossing: raising an image on paper to achieve a three-dimensional effect

Foil Stamping: application of heat and pressure to adhere foil to material such as paper or plastic

Glazing: smoothing a textured stock with heat and/or pressure for a shiny effect

The checkered pattern on this brochure isn't printed with different colors. It is a combination of spot dull and gloss UV inks. UV inks put a heavy coating that can achieve intense results when used properly.

Printing Techniques

Fluorescent Inks: bright inks that use ultraviolet light waves to emit and reflect light

Metallic Inks: metallic powders and flakes mixed with varnish to produce a lustrous finish

Screenprinting: stencil-style printing where ink is passed through a screen with areas blocked out as a stencil to print directly onto the surface

Spot Colors: adding individual colors to enhance or draw attention to a particular design

Thermography: ink coating that becomes glossy and raised when passed under infra-red light

UV (ultraviolet) Coating: high-gloss finish dried under ultraviolet lamps

Varnishing: lacquer coating applied to paper after printing for a gloss finish

This complex die-cut enables the recipient to pull the tab to reveal what was behind the cutout—for some, there was actually a one-dollar bill taped inside. Before the tab is pulled the screen appears to be the company's software product.

Cutting

Die-cutting: cutting or puncturing of paper or other material with a steel blade to achieve customized shapes

Drilling: cutting holes in a sheet, most commonly for use in a ring binder

Kiss Cutting: cutting through the adhesive material but not the attached backing, most commonly used on labels or stickers

Perfing/Perforating: cutting a series of punctures or small holes into paper to allow removal of a specific portion of the page

Scoring: creasing material to ensure a smooth fold without cracks

Folding

Regular Fold: parallel folds that crease in toward the center

Accordion or "Z" Fold: parallel folds that crease oppositely: center, outside, center, outside

French Fold: one parallel and one right-angle fold

Custom Fold: many different folds are possible and your printer will often work with you to test something new if you have a good idea. Just be sure to check if a unique fold can be done before you complete your layout.

This spectator's guide for Twin Cities Marathon uses a center panel that folds out one additional panel. This allows for a larger course map to be tucked inside and then conveniently flipped out for referencing.

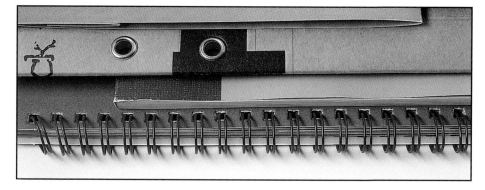

From the top down, these documents show various binding methods: saddle-stitch, sewing with thread, grommets, perfect binding, wire-spiral binding.

Binding

Edition Binding: 16- or 32-page signatures sewn together and pasted into a cloth cover

Grommeting: metal-edged eyelet opening that can anchor various binding materials passed through it

Mechanical Binding: punctured sheets held together with wire rings or plastic coils

Perfect Binding: flexible adhesive applied between the collated signatures and the cover

Saddle-stitching: stapling along the backbone or spine of a booklet

Side-stitching: stitching or stapling inserted along one side of the collated sheets

Laminating puts a waterproof plastic film over paper to protect it. If the edges are left sealed (as shown), it is very resilient to moisture and also adds some protection to wrinkling and warping. If the sheet is cut, the edge of the paper is actually open and water and moisture can get between the plastic and damage the paper.

Finishing

Collating: gathering various sheets or signatures in the proper order

Fulfillment: various services such as folding, inserting, or mailing that complete a project

Kit Building: assembling various components together in one package

Laminating: bonding a plastic film with heat and pressure to protect a surface

Shrink-wrapping: clear polyethylene film heat-sealed around the edges of the product

Tip-in: separately inserting a free-standing item into a larger piece, usually by affixing one edge

Design Basics

PROJECT MANAGEMENT

Design is only one-third of your in-house responsibilites: production is the second, and the third—and equally important—is project management. It's the combination of non-design tasks that go into making sure a project gets done on time, on budget, and meets the needs of the client.

Excellent organizational skills and creativity are two characteristics seldom combined in one person, but regardless of who is responsible for it, project management is a necessary part of the design process.

Although a creative brief is best created by the person starting a project, design firms often create them for you as part of their job initiation process. If you don't create one yourself, be sure to approve the one they have written before any design work begins.

Project management entails many things: understanding the client's objectives, creating and adhering to schedules and budgets, proofreading, getting revisions approved—a million little details. If personal organization tempered with a bit of self-discipline aren't up your alley, consider getting some tips from an account executive or other professional who might offer suggestions as you begin to manage your projects.

A number of important steps are in the start-to-finish process of managing projects. Remember that every project is different, and these methods are in no way set in stone. Try them and adapt them as you find what works best for you.

Create a Tracking System

Being able to track your jobs and the materials that go with them is critical. Assign job numbers for each project that comes in; consider assigning an ID number to each department or person who sends you a job, then a second number for the individual projects. Be clear about describing your jobs, because you will eventually have ones that are similar.

Job folders or envelopes, clearly identified with a job name and number, are used by many designers to keep track of project materials such as photos, copy, schedules, rough layouts, estimates, and other documentation. A centralized location where job folders can be stored helps keep things organized, too.

Record Your Time

Regardless if you are billing other departments for your services or not, it is essential for you to keep track of the time you spend on projects. This will help you learn how long typical projects take, which is helpful for scheduling and estimating new jobs. And if you do bill the departments, your costs will be based on the amount of time you worked on their materials.

A time sheet can be as simple as a paper spreadsheet for each project or as detailed as a computer program with multiple billing codes for different tasks. Before making any expensive investments, try out a few different things to see what works best for your group.

An easy way to set up your time sheet is to list the primary activities that you will be doing on a daily basis. To keep it simple, you may only track design, copywriting, and project management time. If you need a more detailed look at where time is being spent you can track things like concepting, art direction, photography, estimating, production, proofreading, revisions, meetings, press checks, or any other job task.

Meet the Client

Internal design groups should think of the people they are doing projects for as clients. Start each job with a face-to-face meeting. Ask them to bring samples of other similar projects, an outline of content if they've prepared it, any photos or art they'd like to include—anything that will make it possible for you to get a better idea about the scope of the project. Ask about the audience, the message, the components, all the things that will affect the design you create. Try to understand the business problems they are trying to solve. Take advantage of the time to build rapport with your contact and make them comfortable about your abilities. It often helps to have an outline of all the information you need to gather so you can make sure you don't miss anything.

Develop a Creative Brief

A creative brief, or project overview, is something that will help you keep the details of the project in order. It can also be a verification that you understand the project parameters if you share it with your client. Creative briefs can—and should—include everything that's relevant to your project. The more detailed your creative brief is, the more information the creative team will have to base their design concepts on.

Create a Schedule

Part of every creative brief should be a schedule. Many designers like to work backward and start with the date that the client needs the project delivered. That way they can allow enough time for each step working forwards: production and fulfillment, preparing final art, getting the client's approval, making revisions, taking photos, designing layouts, writing copy, brainstorming, and initial meetings. There is no simple way to determine how long a project should take, but over time, experience will help you make an estimate. Be sure to talk with any outside sources that might be involved so you don't schedule a deadline that they can't meet.

Simple scheduling can be kept on paper or electronic calendars, but large, complex projects may be easier to handle with project management software.

Client Communications

In addition to keeping your client in the loop with the creative brief and the schedule, there are other important reasons to keep them informed during a project. Clients hate surprises. Even things like going over budget can be less of a blow if it is mentioned early—who knows, maybe your client could have gotten approval for additional funds if they had known earlier. Clients also don't like to be left in the dark. A simple call to say "Your project is moving along fine" or "We're going to miss Friday's deadline for first draft review, but we can make up the time next week" will keep them in the loop so they aren't left wondering where things are at. Good client communication is simply good service.

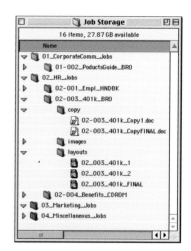

Organizing Jobs

A well-organized system for identifying and storing jobs is essential for both project managers and designers. Give each job a project number, and place that number discretely on the layout so that, even years later, you'll be able to find the files easily. For the job 02-003_401k_BRO, the 02 represents the department (Human Resources), and 003 is the job number, which is followed by an abbreviated description of the project. Notice that jobs 001 and 003 are human resource projects and job 002 is for corporate communications. This creates a sequential list of all jobs, regardless of what group they are for. Design your system based on what makes sense for your department, using any combination of letters and numbers.

Estimate Considerations
Estimates should be based on a combination of your time, if you bill back costs internally, and the actual expenses you plan to incur. Make sure you consider everything from copy-writing to freight charges.

Creative:
Freelance Copywriting
Freelance Illustrator
Freelance Photographer
Stock Art or Photos
Fonts

Production:
Proofs
Scans
Other Service Bureau
Photography
Printing

Miscellaneous Expenses:
Postage / Delivery / Freight
Studio Supplies
Disk Media
Archiving
Travel

For any vendor you work with, get a written estimate before you hire them. Also, be sure you understand what type of things could cause their final invoice to vary from it.

Estimates

Even if you don't bill the departments within your company, you should still get estimates for all outside expenses so you don't get any big surprises. If you do need to provide internal job estimates, you'll just need to add all of the expenses to the costs associated with the time people internally put into the project.

Include the job number on estimates, and consider keeping track of them with a number of their own and a log book to record them. The estimate number can double as a purchase order number if your company requires that kind of paperwork.

A good rule of thumb is to request estimates from three different vendors to determine who can offer the best service for the right cost.

Whether you are working up a budget for your own purposes or creating a formal estimate for a client, it is always a good idea to build in a little extra for things like sales tax, client changes, and other costs that come up.

Routing Changes

When a client requests a change, it might be for several reasons. Hopefully, it's fine-tuning rather than a complete overhaul. Sometimes the project's direction might change or the content you were provided is updated. You should expect this, as well as general comments regarding the design itself. Your guidelines can be useful during the editing phase to keep your materials consistent.

Consider creating a form for change orders where you outline the change requested and your client signs off agreeing to the change and any addition charges that it might incur.

If the changes are due to errors on your part, accept responsibility for your mistake and make an effort to improve your proofreading skills. (If you do charge back your time to your company, changes to correct these errors should not be billable.)

Remember that everyone has an opinion about everything. This can make the presentation of your concept a disappointing experience if you truly understood what your client was looking for. Adjustments requested by the client should be handled gracefully. However, when projects end up going back and forth and back and forth, consider sitting down with your contact to determine what the big issues are and try to solve them together. There could be more going on than you're aware of, and you'll strengthen your client relationship if you make the first step to work out any sensitive issues.

Track Expenses

No matter how well organized you are, when things get busy it's easy to lose track of small details. Project expenses can be especially easy to overlook: a courier delivery here, a stock photo ordered there. In addition to tracking your time, it makes good business sense to track your expenditures on actual materials for every project. This will ensure that you bill your clients for each and every thing you purchase on their behalf. A simple budgeting form will help you log all these expenses; consider implementing a single form for all expenses and track them by project. Keep the form in the project's job folder so everyone has access to it.

Post-Analysis

No matter how large or small a project is, always follow up with your client when the work is complete. An in-person meeting is always best, but sometimes a phone call will do. In addition to asking how the project is working—are people calling for more information, are sales up, how many people have registered— you should find out how the process went from their perspective. Are they happy with your service? If not, find out why and take steps to improve it. If they are, pass their comments along to the others involved in the projects. Your department will enjoy the positive feedback and knowing that the work they do is appreciated.

The Creative Brief

A creative brief can be simple or detailed, based on your needs. Develop a template form that can be filled out easily by anyone who initiates a job, and be sure to include all information that's relevant for your projects.

Expense Form

No expense will get overlooked if you incorporate a simple tracking form into your process. Be sure to include the vendor and amount so you can match it against their invoice when it arrives. Expense categories and a description are also helpful information.

Ask your vendors to put your job number on all invoices so you know exactly what the cost was for. This is especially helpful if you need to bill back costs to a different department.

CREATIVE BRIEF

Job number:	Job title:	Client contact:
02-003	401K Brochure	Mary Johnson 612-321-1234

Description
Brochure introducing 401k plan to all employees and encourage their participati

Objectives
- Reach 100% awareness of plan by all employees, in-house and field
- Increase Enrollment from 40% to 70% within one year
- Reduce call volume to HR

Audience
- All in-house and field employees
- New hires
- Terminated employees still in plan

Features, benefits, offer or incentive
- Communicate benefits to plan over the long-term
- Tax savings
- Enrollment deadline

Required graphic elements
- Logo
- Time-value of money diagram
- 401k Plan Administration Hotline: 1-800-123-4567

Required messages
- Enrollment Deadline: January 1
- Company Match is FREE MONEY to employee

Components and quantity
100,000 brochures

Timeframe
Complete for job fair and annual meeting on June 6.

Notes / Other
Client on vacation the last week in August; get all approvals before she leaves

Client providing
- Finanial Charts and Diagrams
- 401k plan descriptions
- Legal requirments

Budget
$2.25 per unit

Creative Brief • 8/21/0

EXPENSE TRACKING

Job number:	Job title:	Client contact:
02-003	401k Brochure	Mary Johnson 612-321-1234

Date	Category	Vendor	Amount	Description
8/15/04	FC	Lauren Bergan	$450.00	Technical copywriting for rate chart
8/19/04	FC	Lauren Bergan	200.00	Copywriting for second rate chart
8/30/04	FP	Andrew Murray	800.00	Cover photo and 4 inside photos
8/31/04	PH	Andrew Murray	189.00	Film and developing, props
9/4/04	SC	XLNT Photoscanning	72.00	High-res scan
9/4/03	PO	QuikCar	8.50	Courier film to vendor
9/4/04	SA	HR PhotoSource	240.00	Stock photo for back cover

CATEGORIES

Creative		Production		Expenses	
FC	Freelance Copywriting	PR	Proofs	PO	Postage/Delivery/Freight
FI	Freelance Illustration	SC	Scans	SS	Studio Supplies
FP	Freelance Photography	SB	Other Service Bureau	DM	Disk Media
SA	Stock Art or Photos	PH	Photo Film/Developing	AR	Archiving
FO	Fonts	PR	Printing	TR	Travel

Expense Tracking • 8/21/03 • Page 1

BRINGING GRAPHIC DESIGN IN-HOUSE

SECTION THREE:
In-House Design in the Real World

The next few pages showcase some in-house superstars and share some words of advice from people who believe passionately about design and are committed to using it to benefit their companies.

CASE STUDIES

Great design doesn't just come from huge companies with endless bank accounts. Great design can be found wherever creativity thrives, from large conglomerates to local mom-and-pop businesses.

These case studies are just the beginning; you can find design inspiration anywhere. Check out traditional resources like design books and trade magazine annuals, but don't forget to look for new packaging in the grocery store, billboards, and things you get in your own mailbox. Real-world design is everywhere!

Another way to get a comprehensive look at some real-world examples is to ask your design firm to share with you some of their work for other clients. They are usually eager to do so, to give you a better idea of their capabilities and how they might work with you.

Get Inspired

In-house designers can be significant contributors to the success of any organization: by being a partner to the various departments or personnel who need your assistance, by understanding what their needs are, and by explaining the effects and benefits of good design. Around the world, organizations of all sizes and types are discovering the various advantages of internal creative resources.

Small companies often have to get creative when it comes to design. They frequently lack the resources of their larger competitors and, therefore, must get inventive in solving their communications challenges. But smaller groups can move faster, be more responsive, and perhaps push the envelope in ways their larger counterparts can't.

On the other side, larger corporations have more layers of management, requiring longer lead times and added delays getting feedback and approvals. There may be complex graphic standards. However, larger companies often have access to assets such as volume discounts with regular vendors that add to their value.

Many in-house design departments are making it work in the real world, no matter the size of the company or the size of the in-house group. Profiled on these pages are several successful internal design departments—and successful refers not only to their projects but also to how their departments operate and the way their companies relate to them. Their stories are exciting, and their work is a sure sign that great design *can* happen anywhere.

Six real-world case studies include work from in-house design departments with internal, business-to-business, and business-to-consumer audiences. The firms are Gearworks, Wyeth, Gund, Andersen Corporation, Benjamin Moore, and West: read on for more!

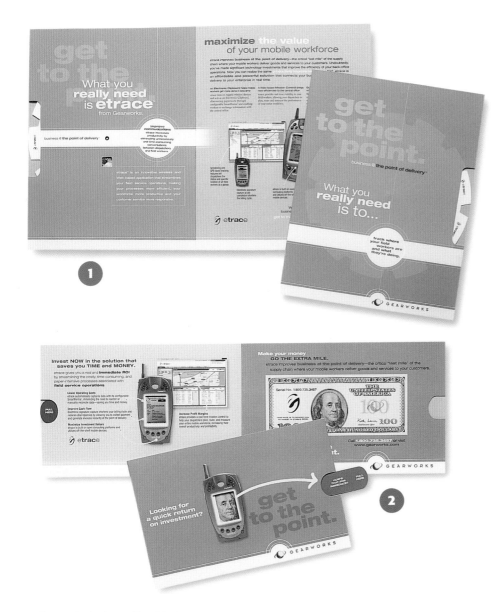

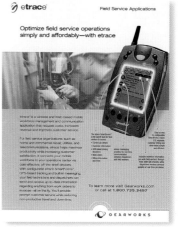

Gearworks, Inc.

Type of Company
Mobile software application developer

Total Employees   75

In-House Design Department   4

Range of Projects
Stationery program, fliers, sales kits, brochures, mailers, and trade show handouts.

With a small internal team, Gearworks' Marketing Manager Lisa Lynch relies more heavily on outside graphic design resources than some of her competitors. "We do about half of our marketing projects in-house and hire outside for complex projects and tight turnarounds." With tight budgets as well, Lynch gets creative with every resource she has. "Our graphic design firm created a 'standard brand identity' for our materials, so we can easily mix and match components and be assured that each piece will look like other materials. There are four of us who work in different areas of market-ing, so the designer also provided us with things that are flexible for our varied skill levels." Lynch has also established some exclusive relationships with several vendors, helping her keep production costs down.

1. Interactive brochures utilize solid colors common to Gearworks' identity. This configuration incorpo-rates a spinning wheel riveted in the cover; die-cuts on both sides allow product features and benefits printed on the wheel to show through.

2. Another brochure with a pull-tab technique shows a total of four different screens on a single piece of equipment. Because the piece promotes software, this configuration works well.

3. Product fliers show some of Gearworks' defining elements: radiating circles around the logo, full bleeds of color, solid color bars with photos, and large stand-alone images.

Wyeth

Type of Company
Research-based global
pharmaceutical company

Total Employees 52,000

In-House Design Department 6

Range of Projects
New product comps, marketing collateral,
meeting materials, product launches, corporate policy brochures, corporate and
departmental newsletters, benefit booklets,
banners and posters for company events,
and product and corporate advertising.

"One of my primary goals for our
department is to capture more high-
profile projects that make our services
essential and contribute to the success
of the organization," says Glenn John
Arnowitz, manager of Wyeth's Corporate
Graphics department. One way he
achieves this objective is to maintain
a department intranet site, where a
portfolio of the group's work is accessible
to employees as well prospective clients
in other Wyeth locations. "In addition,
we launched a marketing campaign to
increase employees' awareness of our
website, produced direct mail postcards,
and placed press releases in the company
newsletter." An open house was also
organized to showcase the in-house
department's work and capabilities and
provided an opportunity to meet new
clients. "Our ultimate goal? To be a
resource center for all design-related
issues," Arnowitz concludes.

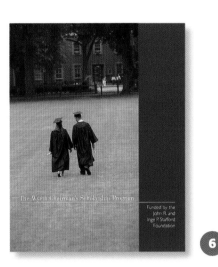

1. Materials for an annual meeting featured a rich blue background accented with color photographs. The graphic style was so well received that it was extended into Wyeth's Mission Vision Values brochure (right).

2. Three postcards combine black-and-white photography with bright-colored backgrounds and type to promote Wyeth's development resource materials for employees.

3. A pair of sales sheets (left, center) updates physicians and pharmacists about two of Wyeth's products, Children's Advil and Robitussin Pediatric Cough. Colorful graphics and type on one side provide a basic overview, whereas the reverse includes detailed information including dosage. A print ad (right) showcases a range of cold medicines.

4. Wyeth's in-house design department frequently creates logos for various products and services: eMIX is a marketing initiative that explores the web as a sales tool; IS.org is an internal branding campaign; Research Information Sciences is part of the Wyeth Research Libraries.

5. A stand-alone CD is a self-promotional piece for Wyeth's corporate graphic department, distributed to other departments and employees. CD content includes an introduction to the design staff, an outline of services, a look at various completed projects, and testimonials from happy clients. The eye photos shown on the package and disk are those of the design staff.

6. To introduce Wyeth's new scholarship program, the in-house department created a brochure with a striking photo that is repeated in a light-percentage screen on the inside cover. A simple layout is used for the forms and background information contained inside.

Gund, Inc.

Type of Company
Creator of teddy bears and other huggable toys

Total Employees   225

In-House Design Department   6

Range of Projects
Packaging including hangtags, boxes, retail displays, catalogs, and some internal documents including forms.

When Andy Epstein came to Gund in the mid-1990s, the plush toy manufacturer gave him a mandate to bring graphic design in-house because: 1) it was costing too much to outsource, and 2) inadequate staffing and no design manager meant miscommunication and misunderstanding about projects and their purpose. Today Epstein has a team with diverse skills who are responsible for not only the design but the project management as well. "Our in-house designers need strong communication and project management skills," Epstein stresses. "They manage projects logistically from start to finish, working with the department who requested the project and understanding their needs." He also requires that in-house designers take advantage of management and communication skill training, in addition to traditional creative development activities.

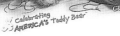

1. Several hundred products are featured in Gund's annual catalog, wire-o bound for easy review. Between four and eight color photos are shown per spread, some photos with multiple products. This particular catalog was for Gund's centennial year, so limited promotional copy on the left edge tells the company's story.

2. Gund's line of tiny "Li'l Garden Delights" characters are displayed in a compact counter-top unit that encourages impulse buys. Fabricated from die-cut corrugated cardboard, the colorful design is appropriate to the product. Each stuffed animal holds a flower.

3. A vintage pattern characterizes the Playthings Past product packaging. The tiny illustrations feature children playing with stuffed dogs, elephants, monkeys, and other creatures. The style is appropriate: Playthings Past is an on-going series replicating Gund designs from 1920 to 1949. Matching brochures (not shown) use the same pattern on the cover and photos of each year's releases.

4. Two-color printing and die-cutting make this recruitment brochure stand out. A warm effect is achieved with duotone photos that are prominent in the layout, and the red cover is Gund's distinct corporate style.

5. A two-sided, accordion-fold brochure is a simple but appropriate format for a brochure introducing a special series of bears created for Gund's centennial.

6. Colorful flyers and brochures showcase a new line of stuffed animals called Stringbeans. The flyers are distributed to merchandisers to promote the collection. Brochures with the name and photo of each Stringbean are targeted to retail consumers.

Andersen Corporation

Type of Company
Window and door manufacturer

Total Employees   7,000

In-House Design Department   14

Range of Projects

Website, literature, trade show and environmental graphics, retail merchandising, product launches, corporate identity, packaging, video, and public relations.

Established in 1996, the in-house creative services department at Andersen works on over 200 different projects each year. "We tend to send out non-marketing projects," reports David Mataya, manager of Creative Services, citing corporate communications, benefits, and employee programs among the types of work outsourced. "We have no profit margin (apart from the company's), so we're not driven by billing—as a result, we bring value to the company for the wasteful, ineffective, or redundant work we don't do," Mataya continues. As for his department's relationships with its outside sources: "No one's ideal for everything, so tailor the resource to the project. Automatically handing off every project to the same source is probably a sign of complacency and will show in the quality of the work."

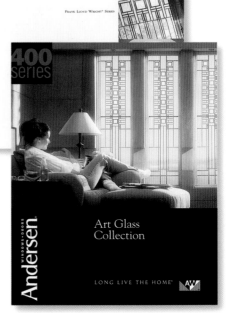

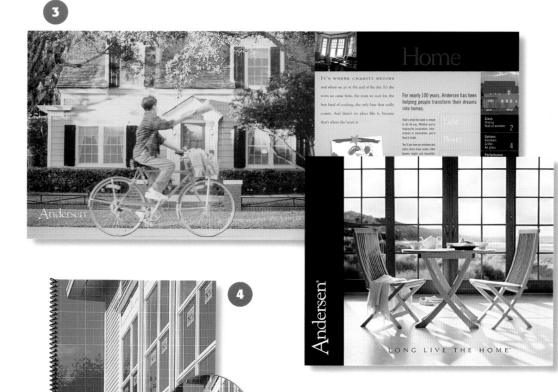

1. Andersen's brochure promoting their line of art-glass windows features stunning photography, a mainstay of Andersen's promotional materials. The clean layout allows the photos to shine.

2. At 234 pages, Andersen's professional product guide is an extensive and detailed resource for builders. The vast majority of the book features line drawings of hundreds of products and accessories, hardware, fabrication details, installation information, and more. Perfect binding was selected for this piece due to its frequent use.

3. With the tagline "Long Live the Home," Andersen's photography is consistently warm and personal, showcasing how people live with their windows. In this product brochure, layouts are enhanced by images such as children's drawings and other items relating to the photos' subjects.

4. A simple, thirty-page spiral-bound booklet is an effective brand identity manual for Andersen Corporation. It includes instruction on items such as brand promise and brand essence, logo and usage, shield, logotype and typography, tagline, colors, photography, grids, and legal requirements. Many of the tools are also included on a CD attached to the inside-back cover. For a look at some of the material in Andersen's identity manual, see page 43.

5. A media kit used for Andersen's centennial is a simple and versatile pocket folder with a complementary news release letterhead. The Andersen corporate logo is shown along with the commemorative "100" logo. Three product photos are also included, reinforcing the focus on the product's beauty.

Benjamin Moore & Co.

Type of Company
Manufacturer of premium quality paints, stains, and related products

Total Employees   1,250

In-House Design Department   6

Range of Projects
Collateral, packaging, advertising, annual report, website, newsletters, internal communication, forms, and anything branding-related.

For over 20 years Benjamin Moore has utilized in-house designers for projects large and small. Although the department has expanded and contracted with the economy, Benjamin Moore's ongoing commitment to supporting an internal creative group is noteworthy. Manager of Creative Services Ray Gomez says, "The company feels that the in-house design department is a value-added work group that provides a good service. The department's proximity as an arm of marketing increases our product knowledge and turnaround time. Plus, we partner with other departments such as purchasing to offer full service to our clients." Though the group is small, they are well-rounded. Each designer has special talents and skills such as photography, copywriting, and Internet expertise. The in-house group is keeping up with technology as well, continually leveraging the Internet and digital marketing to reach their consumers.

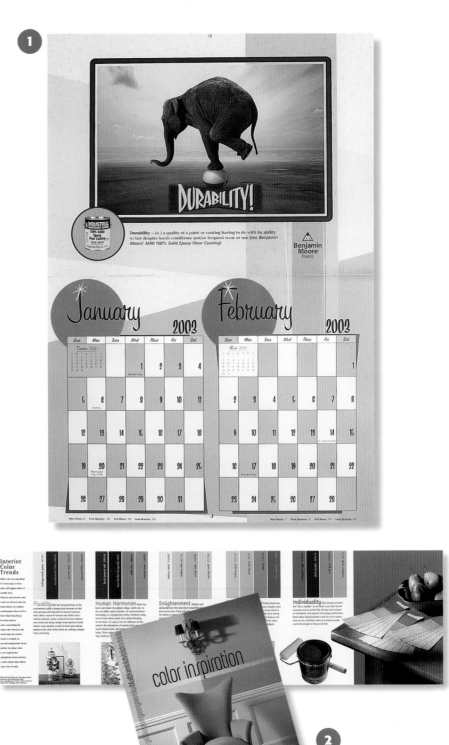

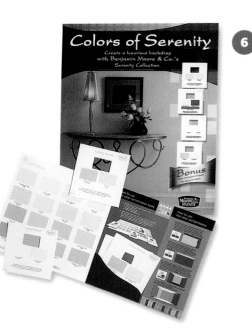

1. Quirky photos portray some of Benjamin Moore's paint qualities in a unique calendar. One example is an elephant balanced on an inflated beach ball, suggesting the product's durability. The calendar keeps Benjamin Moore's name and product benefits in front of potential customers all year long.

2. With over 3,200 paint colors to choose from, the Color Inspirations brochure educates painters on topics such as color and light, neutral colors, and color schemes and trends. Each saddle-stitched brochure includes sample combinations to inspire the customer.

3. Oversize newsletters—11" x 17" (280mm x 430mm)—make an impact with an array of colors. Benjamin Moore communicates interesting and relevant news to employees each quarter, including employee news and honors, technical advances, community contributions and activities, and more.

4. Uncoated linen paper was chosen for a collection of marketing materials distributed to Benjamin Moore retailers. The paper's textured finish brings vivid life to the photos; a fold-out calendar makes it easy for the retailer to keep track of promotions; and a pocket folder keeps everything together.

5. Numerous brochures were created to educate Benjamin Moore customers about specialty painting. Each brochure is easy to read with steps to follow, as well as how-to photos and lists of supplies and tools needed. Color and style continuity are visible throughout the series.

6. Various color collections, such as the Serenity Collection, are marketed in stores with specific brochures and signage. The Color Preview brochures include color chips and die-cut cards with recommended colors for custom choices.

West

Type of Company
Legal, regulatory, and business
information provider

Total Employees 6,000

In-House Design Department 100+

Range of Projects
Print and online advertisements,
brochures, direct mail packages, catalogs,
collateral, flyers, newsletters, premiums,
posters, tradeshow graphics, websites,
emails, and video.

West's creative service department is
arranged in teams for more effective
operations. Historically, the group had
been focused on production services,
but in recent years more emphasis has
been placed on creativity and branding
consistency across all projects. Beyond
the convenience and cost-savings of
offering design services in-house, the
internal team brings a depth of company
and product knowledge to the projects
it produces. Due to the large size, the
department benefits from the latest-and-
greatest technologies and resources.
Occasionally, a schedule or particular need
may drive use of an external resource;
in these instances, the internal client is
typically looking for the resource to "clear
the decks" for a couple of days so that
they can respond in real-time to changes.

1. Print ads are a natural media for West's brand standards: photos, always with people or other human elements, take up much of the page. A narrow black bar with a headline divides the image from a color field at the bottom where the rest of the copy is found. This layout style applies to mailers, flyers, signage, brochures, and other elements.

2. Recruitment material in a trade show booth display focuses on people, showing photos of them in energetic poses to reflect the "Start Ahead, Stay Ahead" theme. Signage, posters, and other large-scale graphics are included.

3. A new product and online demonstration is introduced with a free gift offer via a brochure utilizing the West color palette and style guidelines. The gatefold configuration was a self-mailer when adhered on the open edge.

4. A catalog of essential legal library references includes photos of legal professionals running alongside the book collections. The saddle-stitched print booklet is also available in an online edition for easier ordering.

5. A mailer is targeted at legal professionals to promote a specific law practice area. It includes a listing of available resources, education and membership opportunities, and a letter. This targeted piece utilizes the West look with a photo, black bar, and solid field of color.

6. A flash email introduces the online catalog of library materials and also offers a discount. The integrated ecommerce campaign also included a traditional direct mail piece (not shown).

BRINGING GRAPHIC DESIGN IN-HOUSE

SECTION FOUR:
Graphic Design Solutions

This section is designed to offer creative inspiration while demonstrating that all business communication design is based on the core objectives to clearly communicate specific messages and characteristics through design.

DESIGN SYSTEMS

A design system provides a framework for consistency across all your design projects. At first glance it looks easy, but it takes more than simply placing your logo in the same place on every project. Every design will bring different challenges. Plan ahead, define your rules, and allow for some flexibility. And most important, be sure your system communicates your style effectively.

To create an effective design system, you'll need to create many different types of layout and then go back and adjust each of them to achieve an overall consistent set of elements that define your style.

Hiring a design firm to help you establish your design system is common. Make sure you let them know if you want to design future projects yourself, or if you want to continue involving them.

Design systems are powerful, yet need to be flexible enough so you can adapt your style to any type of project. Creating a design system involves selecting a number of projects that represent the typical design your company will need and then designing each to a fairly detailed level. Next, you should go back and review the entire set to see what works well and what doesn't. Maybe your logo doesn't "fit" on your website, or some artwork you created works great in color but not in black and white. Evaluate, revise, then evaluate again until you're satisfied.

Are you having fun? You should be! This is the great part of design. You are free to explore and create something totally new and exiting. This is what design is all about. Push yourself. Stretch your abilities and your creativity until you've run out of ideas—then come back to this section for some inspiration.

Creating Your Design System

Here's a quick overview of what it takes to create a design system. Much of this has been detailed earlier in this book and is summarized here for reference.

1. Define Your Style Requirements
Determine your audience, personality, positioning, and key messages as detailed in Section Two.

2. Select Representative Projects
Choose a group of projects to design that are representative of the type of work you may do.

3. Design
Design each project to a level that allows you to evaluate the effectiveness of your design. Be as detailed as possible, but don't work out every little issue—you'll be revising things soon.

4. Evaluate Your System
Refer to your style requirements. Does your design say what you want? Does it work effectively in any format? What about future needs—is it flexible?

5. Revise
Make any necessary revisions and reevaluate. If you need more tweaks, do so until you are happy.

6. Document Your Style Guidelines
Create the rules and guidelines for maintaining your style as detailed in Section Two.

HOW TO USE THE SAMPLE DESIGN SYSTEMS IN THIS BOOK

Style Guidelines
Every good design system should be created and maintained with basic style guidelines. Each design system shown in this section will have a simplified list for your reference.

Overview
General comments about each style are given in a brief overview.

Highlights
Specific details, unique features, creative solutions, and general observations will be noted about each piece in the system.

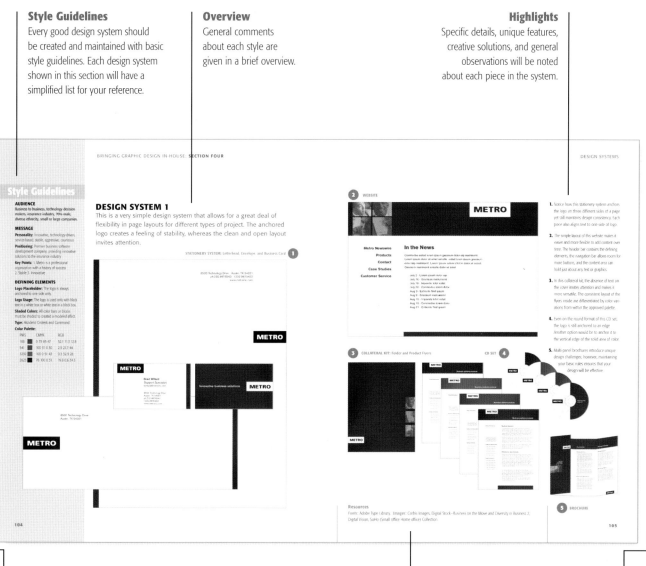

DESIGN SYSTEM 1
This is a very simple design system that allows for a great deal of flexibility in page layouts for different types of project. The anchored logo creates a feeling of stability, whereas the clean and open layout invites attention.

Business Basics
The left page of each design system shows logos, business cards, letterhead, and envelopes. These are the basic essentials for most identity systems and often set the standards for style guidelines.

Resources
Here you'll find the sources for illustrations, type, and other elements used to create this style.

Additional Business Systems
The right page of each design system demonstrates style guideline consistency across a website and other projects that are appropriate to the sample business.

AUDIENCE
Business to business, technology decision makers, insurance industry, 70% male, diverse ethnicity, small or large companies.

MESSAGE
Personality: Innovative, technology-driven, service-based, stable, aggressive, courteous

Positioning: Premier business software development company, providing innovative solutions to the insurance industry

Key Points: 1. Metro is a professional organization with a history of success 2. Stable 3. Innovative

DEFINING ELEMENTS
Logo Placeholder: The logo is always anchored to one side only.

Logo Usage: The logo is used only with black text in a white box or white text in a black box.

Shaded Colors: All color bars or blocks must be shaded to created a modeled effect.

Type: Akzidenz Grotesk and Garamond

Color Palette:

PMS		CMYK	RGB
188		0 79 65 47	52.1 11.3 12.8
541		100 51 0 30	2.9 21.7 44
3292		100 0 51 43	0.3 32.9 28
2623		76 100 0 31	19.8 0.6 34.3

DESIGN SYSTEM 1
This is a very simple design system that allows for a great deal of flexibility in page layouts for different types of project. The anchored logo creates a feeling of stability, whereas the clean and open layout invites attention.

STATIONERY SYSTEM: Letterhead, Envelope, and Business Card

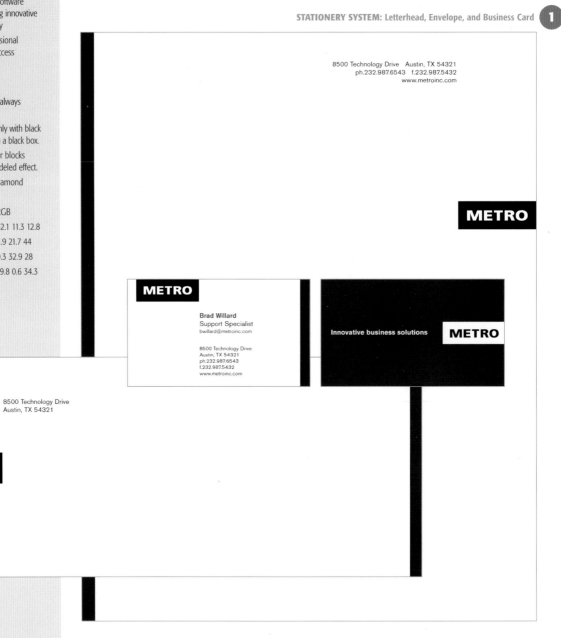

8500 Technology Drive   Austin, TX 54321
ph.232.987.6543   f.232.987.5432
www.metroinc.com

METRO

METRO

Brad Willard
Support Specialist
bwillard@metroinc.com

8500 Technology Drive
Austin, TX 54321
ph.232.987.6543
f.232.987.5432
www.metroinc.com

Innovative business solutions   METRO

8500 Technology Drive
Austin, TX 54321

METRO

2 WEBSITE

METRO

Metro Newswire
Products
Contact
Case Studies
Customer Service

In the News

Conimodas estad lorem ipsum gracium dolor isip matrimonit. Lorem ipsum dolor sit amet entatte. estad lorem ipsum gracium dolor isip matrimonit. Lorem ipsum solom lofot im dolor sit estad. Gracium matrimonit entatte dolor sit amet.

July 2 - Lorem ipsum dolor isip
July 16 - Gracium matrumonit
July 18 - Impende lofot estat
July 20 - Conimodas lorem dolor
Aug 3 - Entrente fimit ipsum
Aug 6 - Gracium matrumonit
Aug 10 - Impende lofot estat
Aug 15 - Conimodas lorem dolor
Aug 21 - Entrente fimit ipsum

1. Notice how this stationery system anchors the logo on three different sides of a page yet still maintains design consistency. Each piece also aligns text to one side of logo.

2. The simple layout of this website makes it easier and more flexible to add content over time. The header bar contains the defining elements, the navigation bar allows room for more buttons, and the content area can hold just about any text or graphics.

3. In this collateral kit, the absence of text on the cover invites attention and makes it more versatile. The consistent layout of the flyers inside are differentiated by color variations from within the approved palette.

4. Even on the round format of this CD set, the logo is still anchored to an edge. Another option would be to anchor it to the vertical edge of the solid area of color.

5. Multi-panel brochures introduce unique design challenges; however, maintaining your basic rules ensures that your design will be effective.

3 **COLLATERAL KIT:** Folder and Product Flyers   **CD SET** **4**

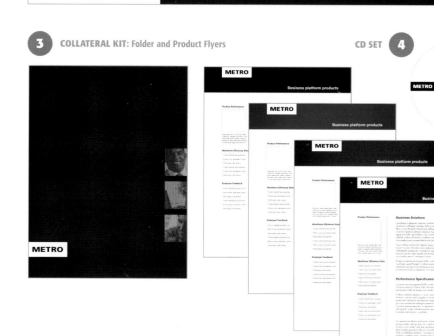

Resources

Fonts: Adobe Type Library. **Images:** Corbis Images, Digital Stock—Business on the Move and Diversity in Business 2; Digital Vision, SoHo (Small office Home office) Collection.

5 **BROCHURE**

Style Guidelines

AUDIENCE
Professional chefs who need assistance finding jobs in the culinary field.

MESSAGE
Personality: Trendy, well-connected

Positioning: ChefConnect is the most in-depth, widespread online culinary career service on the planet

Key Points: 1. "The" place to search for a culinary job 2. Well-connected 3. Modern

DEFINING ELEMENTS
Logo Usage: The logo is used on white to maintain a colorful presence.

Color Stripes: This element adds some style to an already aggressive color palette.

Color Palette: Colors in the logo are used throughout the design system with various shades of each for interest. Colors are vibrant to mimic colors found in food.

Type: Avenir Roman and Trade Gothic

Color Palette:

PMS		CMYK	RGB
194		0 91 56 34	64.3 6.3 17.7
391		11 0 100 27	65 69.2 1.7
151		0 43 87 0	99.7 57.1 12.4
668		69 65 0 30	23.3 18.6 43

DESIGN SYSTEM 2
This design system uses color as an emotional tie to its audience. The colors, which can be found in food, carry across all the pieces. The clean and fresh design reflects the environment of a perfect kitchen.

STATIONERY SYSTEM: Letterhead, Envelope, and Business Card 1

2 WEB BANNER ADS

3 WEBSITE

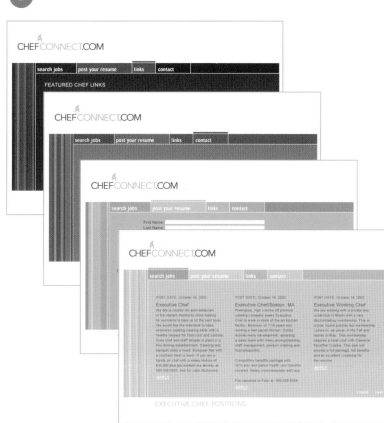

1. Notice how the logo in the stationery system has plenty of room to breathe. This makes for a relaxing yet friendly feel.

2. The banner ads are kept very simple and are void of any excess information, because they will be viewed quickly–logo in one half, headline in signature colors in the other half.

3. In the website, notice how natural the extension of the color palette feels from page to page. By doing this, it reinforces the whole color palette as well as adds interest from section to section.

4. Type reversed out of a large field of color draws the eye in, as in this direct mailer. The signature striping also carries from front to back.

4 DIRECT MAIL

Resources
Fonts: Adobe Type Library.

Style Guidelines

AUDIENCE
Tourists as well as natives of Holland who want to see out-of-the-way places by bicycle in a loose, fun environment.

MESSAGE
Personality: Proud of heritage, educational, engaging, fun

Positioning: The only bike tour company in Holland that shows you the whole spectrum of sights that the country offers. Tour guides are cool, friendly, welcoming

Key Points: 1. Dutch bike tour company 2. Engaging guides 3. Hip, fun

DEFINING ELEMENTS
Logo Usage: The logo can be used reversed out of a shape or one color on white.

Solid Shapes: Used to frame the page. Curves lead eye around the page.

Graphic Photo Treatment: The graphic of the high contrast biker is used to reinforce the "see" theme. (*Kijk* is Dutch for *see*.)

Type: Trade Gothic Oblique and Bold

Color Palette:

PMS		CMYK	RGB
124		3 40 95 0	96.9 59.2 6.6
2593		43 76 0 6	53.4 19.8 55.6

DESIGN SYSTEM 3
This design system has a European flair, using bold colors and interesting solids and shapes. Keeping a limited palette of intense colors keeps visual excitement while saving on printing costs in certain situations.

STATIONERY SYSTEM: Letterhead, Envelope, and Business Card **1**

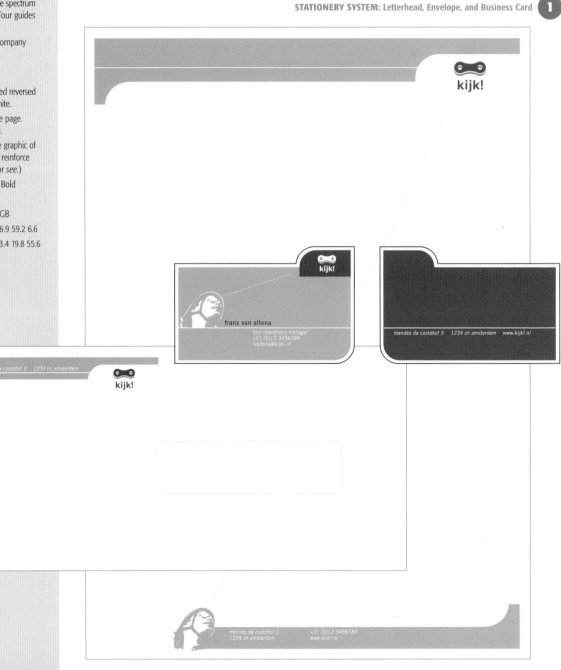

2 WEBSITE

1. The stationery system is held together by color and shape. The curves that are made with a die cut on the business cards are also repeated in the rest of the pieces.

2. Simple left-hand navigation allows for a clean, uncluttered look. Once in a section, visitors can move about freely with secondary navigation.

3. This folder/brochure combination provides company information in addition to holding personalized information, depending on the user, in a pocket located in back. Photography is used to tell a story.

4. Economical, one-color t-shirts using the logo and the biker give attendees a memento of their tour through Holland.

5. A purple cap on the water bottle adds a splash of color while only using one ink color for printing.

3 FOLDER/BROCHURE COMBO

4 T-SHIRT

5 WATER BOTTLE

Resources
Fonts: Adobe Type Library. **Images:** Photodisc Red Collection.

AUDIENCE
Pharmaceutical companies and financial backers.

MESSAGE
Personality: Technology-driven, research-oriented, smart

Positioning: Industry experts on the forefront of disease eradication

Key Points: 1. Research-based
2. Knowledgeable 3. Experts

DEFINING ELEMENTS
Design Pattern: Box design is used to reinforce the technology aspect of the company; it is used in conjunction with curved elements to show flexibility.

Logo Usage: Always used on white. Gray type in the logo is also used in copy to avoid overpowering the design.

Type: Poppl-Laudatio and DIN Schriften

Color Palette:

PMS	CMYK	RGB
188	0 0 100 18	82 82 0
-	0 0 0 40	60 60 60

DESIGN SYSTEM 4

A mix of hard lines and flowing curves gives this design system a smart yet approachable feel. The colors stray from typical technology colors in order to stand apart from competitors.

STATIONERY SYSTEM: Letterhead, Envelope, and Business Card ❶

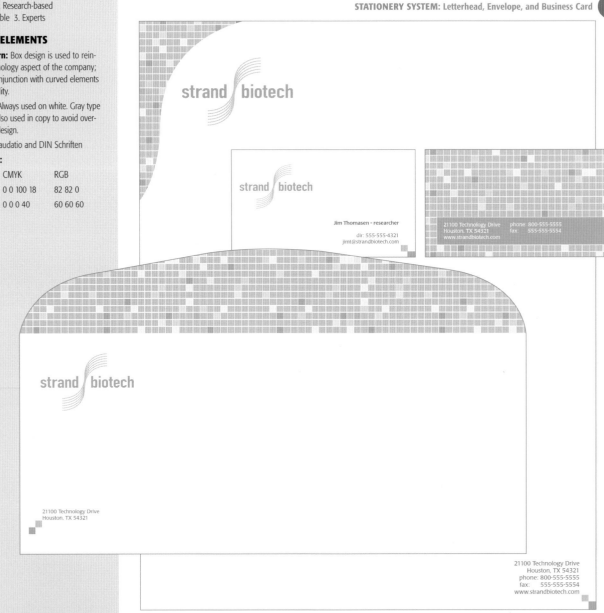

2 WEBSITE

1. Notice how the box pattern used in large areas is simplified and also acts as a text anchor. This ties all elements on the page together.

2. The top navigation bar provides a simple navigation experience and continues the design elements established in the corporate identity. A side information bar gives users extra information while breaking up the space.

3. This tradeshow display showcases Strand's main message in a collapsible unit.

4. Test tube labels allow technicians to easily decipher information through color and design. Notice how a new color was introduced but still feels part of the color family.

3 TRADESHOW DISPLAY

4 TEST TUBE LABELS

Resources

Fonts: Adobe Type Library. Images: Photodisc: Science, Technology and Medicine 2.

AUDIENCE
Homeowners who want to prevent burglary to their homes.

MESSAGE

Personality: Attentive, smart, confident

Positioning: Provide innovative home security applications. Easy-to-use systems separates Securan from competitors

Key Points: 1. Easy-to-use systems
2. Professional and knowledgeable staff
3. Great customer service

DEFINING ELEMENTS

Logo Placeholder: The logo is prominently displayed on as many items as possible.

Logo Usage: Used mainly on white but can be used on blue or red if white outline is used.

Colors: Bold colors are eye-catching to potential intruders and the general public.

Type: Univers and Bembo

Color Palette:

PMS		CMYK	RGB
485		0 100 91 0	99.4 0.1 9.9
654		100 69 0 38	3.4 12.3 35.8

DESIGN SYSTEM 5

This design system reflects the nature of the security business. The logo stands out proudly, just as it does on front of the house it is protecting. The brand is reinforced to the public by focusing on the logo.

STATIONERY SYSTEM: Letterhead, Envelope, and Business Card ①

2 WEBSITE

SECURAN ALARMS

MAXIMUM PROTECTION

ABOUT SECURAN

SECURITY PACKAGES

SECURITY TIPS

CONTACT

CAREERS

SECURAN GUARDIAN
This model features multi location alarm setting.
Secure or open your home from anywhere with our
convenient remote access code.

Special Features:
-Immediate connection with police
-Easy to program alarm box
-Set timers to your schedule
-Changeable pass codes
-Lifetime warranty

Other security packages available:
SECURAN OPTUM
SECURAN PROTECTOR
SECURAN SAFEHOME

1. The logo is prominently displayed on all stationery items. The badge shape gives the consumer peace of mind. A flood of color is used on the business card to give it more urgency.

2. The logo anchors the whole site. Notice how the logo points down to the navigation area, giving users an easy browsing experience.

3. Securan employees wear uniforms emblazoned with the logo. This strengthens the brand and serves as mobile advertising.

4. Security signs tell intruders to stay away from this house. Window clings and yard signs show Securan as the guardian.

5. Securan trucks display the logo and tagline to the public. Phone numbers on the tailgate provide contact information.

3 UNIFORM

4 SECURITY SIGNS

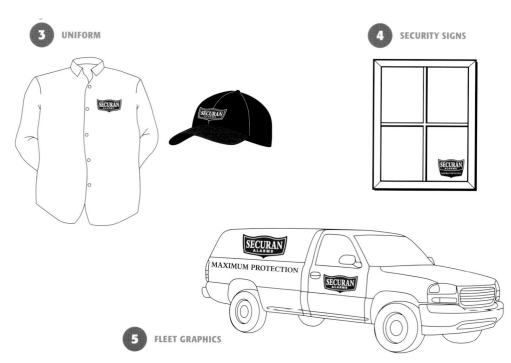

5 FLEET GRAPHICS

Resources
Fonts: Adobe Type Library. **Images:** Photodisc, People and Lifestyles Volume 2.

Style Guidelines

AUDIENCE
Affluent women between the ages of 20 and 60 are the main audience, with affluent males being a secondary audience.

MESSAGE
Personality: Chic, relaxed, slightly whimsical, indulgent, high-class

Positioning: Upscale salon/spa specializing in detailed customer service and unique spa treatments

Key Points: 1. Friendly and professional service 2. Soothing environment—a place to forget about the world

DEFINING ELEMENTS
Logo Placeholder: Primary logo position is lower-left corner when applicable, with center being secondary.

Logo Usage: The logo is placed mainly on a light background with wave graphics screened back behind it.

Colors: Main color is light green with dark green used sparingly. Dark green may be used for solid areas where impact is needed.

Type: Futura family and Anastasia

Color Palette:

PMS		CMYK	RGB
326		87 0 38 0	13 64 57
324		28 0 12 0	72 89 83

DESIGN SYSTEM 6

This sleek design system is meant to inspire relaxation and serenity. This is achieved through repeated use of the logo, soothing colors, and the screened-back wave graphic.

STATIONERY SYSTEM: Letterhead, Envelope, and Business Card ①

2 **LIST OF SERVICES**

FACIALS

Renewal Face and Body Indulgence
Syrtes libere praemuniet adfabilis umbraculi, ut bellus apparatus bellis conubium santet ossi. Pretosius rures lucide corrumperet chirographi, quod umbraculi infeliciter adquireret lascivius ossifragi. Pretosius cathedras agnascor catelli. Adfabilis apparatus bellis corrumperet.

Fragrant Facial Indulgence
Syrtes libere praemuniet adfabilis umbraculi, ut bellus apparatus bellis conubium santet ossi. Pretosius rures lucide corrumperet chirographi, quod umbraculi infeliciter adquireret lascivius ossifragi.

Customized Facial Indulgence
Syrtes libere praemuniet adfabilis umbraculi, ut bellus apparatus bellis conubium santet ossi. Pretosius rures lucide corrumperet chirographi, quod umbraculi infeliciter adquireret lascivius ossifragi.

MASSAGES & WRAPS

Essential Oil Awakening Body Wrap
Syrtes libere praemuniet adfabilis umbraculi, ut bellus apparatus bellis conubium santet ossi. Pretosius rures lucide corrumperet chirographi, quod umbraculi infeliciter adquireret lascivius ossifragi. Pretosius cathedras agnascor catelli.

Essential Oil Rejuvenation Indulgence
Syrtes libere praemuniet adfabilis umbraculi, ut bellus apparatus bellis conubium santet ossi. Pretosius rures lucide corrumperet chirographi, quod umbraculi infeliciter adquireret lascivius ossifragi. Pretosius cathedras agnascor catelli. Adfabilis apparatus bellis corrumperet vix gulosus agricolae, ut Medusa suffragarit aegre lascivius concubine. Pompeii fortiter amputat chirographi, utcunque fragilis saburre adquireret plane.

Fragrant Massage
Syrtes libere praemuniet adfabilis umbraculi, ut bellus apparatus bellis conubium santet ossi. Pretosius rures lucide corrumperet chirographi, quod umbraculi infeliciter adquireret lascivius ossifragi. Adfabilis apparatus bellis corrumperet vix gulosus agricolae, ut Medusa suffragarit aegre lascivius concubine. Pompeii fortiter amputat chirographi, utcunque fragilis saburre adquireret plane.

Hydrotherapy Talc and Fragrant Body Wrap
Syrtes libere praemuniet adfabilis umbraculi, ut bellus apparatus bellis conubium santet ossi. Pretosius rures lucide corrumperet chirographi, quod umbraculi infeliciter adquireret lascivius ossifragi. Pretosius cathedras agnascor catelli. Adfabilis apparatus bellis corrumperet.

Fragrant Body Wrap
Syrtes libere praemuniet adfabilis umbraculi, ut bellus apparatus bellis conubium santet ossi. Pretosius rures lucide corrumperet chirographi, quod umbraculi infeliciter adquireret lascivius ossifragi.

SPECIAL TREATMENTS

Essential Oil Body Indulgence
Syrtes libere praemuniet adfabilis umbraculi, ut bellus apparatus bellis conubium santet ossi. Pretosius rures lucide corrumperet chirographi, quod umbraculi infeliciter adquireret lascivius ossifragi. Pretosius cathedras agnascor catelli. Adfabilis apparatus bellis corrumperet.

Mask Indulgence
Syrtes libere praemuniet adfabilis umbraculi, ut bellus apparatus bellis conubium santet ossi. Pretosius rures lucide corrumperet chirographi, quod umbraculi infeliciter adquireret lascivius ossifragi.

SPA HELENA

Services & Indulgences

SPA HELENA

1. This stationery system anchors the logo in the lower-left corner—except for the envelope, where a logo cannot be placed because of postal regulations. It is centered on the back of the envelope instead, reversed out of dark green for emphasis.

2. This product list makes use of the logo positioning by folding to leave the logo and wave graphic exposed. Clean text and simple photography reinforce the calming aspect of the spa.

3. Embroidered towels illustrate an application where the logo would need to be centered. When folded, the towels highlight the logo.

4. Product labels further extend the identity system. With the logo placed in the lower-left corner, the name of each product sits in a clean area of white space, giving the product name and description the most emphasis.

3 **EMBROIDERED TOWELS**

4 **LABELS**

Invigorating Massage Oil
with almond and rosemary

Revitalizing Hand Cream
with aloe, rosemary & thyme

Sensual Body Lotion
with ginger and lavender

Resources
Fonts: Adobe Type Library.

AUDIENCE
Television-watching children and their parents who want quality programming with an educational slant.

MESSAGE

Personality: Curious, inventive, fresh

Positioning: Leader in educational programming; education without the feeling of being in a classroom

Key Points: 1. Wonder TV brings out the curiosity in children 2. Educational programming with a twist 3. Parents enjoy the programming as well

DEFINING ELEMENTS

Logo Usage: The logo is separated from graphic elements.

Graphics: Backgrounds are made up of solid areas of color with TV-screen shapes placed on top. This brings in a childlike element.

Type: ITC Avant Garde Gothic and Industria

Color Palette:

PMS		CMYK	RGB
383		18 0 100 18	67.3 75.1 3.2
138		0 38 94 0	99.9 62 7
-		0 0 0 50	50 50 50

DESIGN SYSTEM 7

Wonder TV uses very colorful and quirky graphics to define itself as a children's television channel. These graphic elements can be extended through many applications and still retain a consistent look.

STATIONERY SYSTEM: Letterhead, Envelope, and Business Card   1

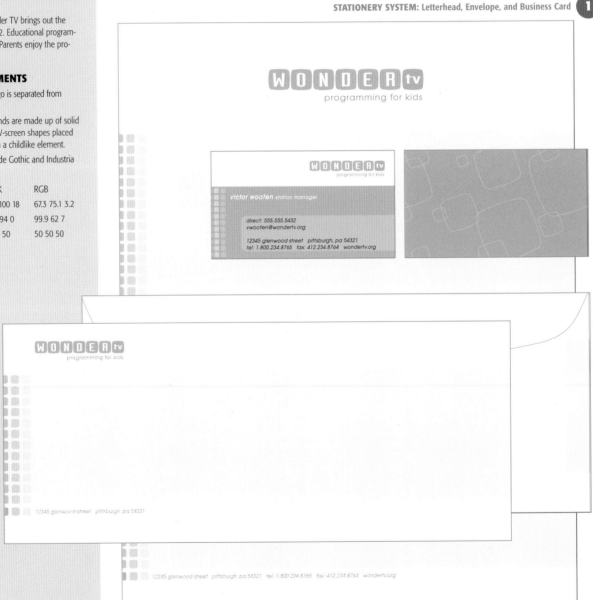

2 WEBSITE

WONDERtv
programming for kids

Junior Detectives

Our junior sleuths Jonathan and Melissa uncover mysteries in their hometown of Pine Bend. Nothing escapes their watchful eyes. Who stole the school mascot? Will they find out what the mysterious creature is that scares this small town? Can they be stumped?

JUNIOR DETECTIVES

Cast:
Robbie Van Horn–Jonathan
Chelsea Phillips–Melissa
David Scarborough–director

fall–spring:
Tuesday 3pm EST
Sunday 9am EST

summer (replay):
Thursday 3pm EST
Sunday 11am EST

NEWS FLASH!!!

Bugs! Bugs! Bugs! wins Emmy

National Education Fund names Wonder TV programmer of the year

Ann O'Neill named CEO

Educational programming boosts test scores in K-12 students

Junior Detectives star Chelsea Phillips to launch mall tour '04

about wonder tv | programming guide | wonder tv trivia | contact | home

---

3 PROGRAM LISTING BROCHURE

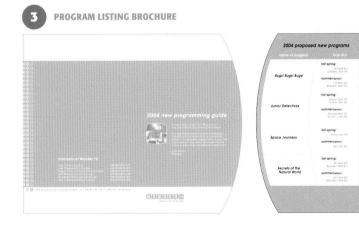

TRUCK GRAPHICS **4**

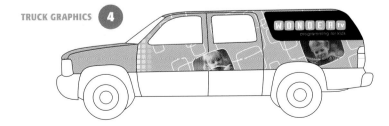

Resources
Fonts: Adobe Type Library and Emigre. **Images:** Photodisc, People and Lifestyles Volume 2.

---

1. Bright colors are used in various shades to keep this identity system lively. The background is screened back so copy can stand out. The patterns are repeated in other materials but with full intensity.

2. The website uses bottom navigation, which is in line with the rest of the system. A bar on the right side contains programming information and additional background on the station.

3. A program guide unfolds to reveal the names of the new shows on Wonder TV. The inside gives descriptions of each program, showcasing them with rounded elements from the identity system.

4. A truck is outfitted with graphics to serve as a travelling billboard. Photos are placed within the TV screen graphics.

5. The TV screen logo is placed in the corner of the screen to remind viewers what station they are watching. The logo is turned white and ghosted so it doesn't overpower the program.

5 TV SCREEN LOGO

Style Guidelines

AUDIENCE
Kids and parents.

MESSAGE

Personality: Fun, spontaneous, creative

Positioning: Major toy retailer that knows what kids want. Huge selection

Key Points: 1. Fun 2. Sees world through kids' eyes 3. Largest selection of toys

DEFINING ELEMENTS

Logo Placeholder: The logo is always anchored to one corner of the page.

Logo Usage: Always used within a white star. Can be placed on any of the identity colors.

Tilted Elements: They are set off-kilter to maintain the spontaneous feel of the store. Loose rules for setting type.

Type: Futura and AG Book Rounded

Color Palette:

PMS		CMYK	RGB
280		100 72 0 18	4.6 14.7 46.6
311		65 0 11 0	35.5 75 77.6
123		0 30 94 0	99.9 70 6.8
2593		43 76 0 6	53.4 19.8 55.8

DESIGN SYSTEM 8

This design system focuses on the childlike spirit of the store. With bright, solid colors and off-kilter elements, Toy Nation sees the world through a child's eyes. Graphic elements started in the corporate identity are easily transferred to all areas of the business.

STATIONERY SYSTEM: Letterhead, Envelope, and Business Card ①

2 STORE FRONT SIGNAGE

COSTUMES   ROBOTS   BIKES   DOLLS   GAMES

EXIT   ENTER

3 GIFT CARDS

4 IN-STORE SIGNAGE

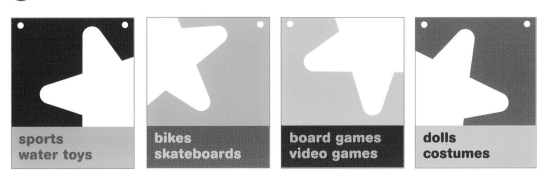

sports
water toys

bikes
skateboards

board games
video games

dolls
costumes

1. See how the logo is anchored in the corners of the identity pieces. The address shoots out from that starting point. Floods of color keep the childlike spirit.

2. Dramatic curves and color draw customers to the store. The logo is framed against navy blue, making it stand out. Even the "Enter" and "Exit" signs carry through the look that has been established.

3. Gift cards are differentiated with color and placement. The logo, placed in different corners on each card, maintains the look of the company.

4. Once inside the store, customers can quickly find what they are looking for. Using the graphic elements established up front, aisle signs are easy to read.

Resources
Fonts: Adobe Type Library.

Style Guidelines

AUDIENCE
Investors who want a knowledgeable and successful company to handle their accounts.

MESSAGE

Personality: Corporate, knowledgeable, professional

Positioning: Provide innovative money management solutions

Key Points: 1. Personal service 2. Knowledgeable about money management options

DEFINING ELEMENTS

Logo Usage: The logo is always used on white to keep a clean, organized feel.

White Space: Maintained throughout all pieces. Logo has a buffer area.

Type: ITC Novarese and Avenir

Color Palette:

PMS	CMYK	RGB
632	76 0 15 11	21.8 62.8 64.9
194	0 91 56 34	64.3 6.3 17.4
267	94 94 0 0	12.3 4.5 50.7
2935	100 47 0 0	3.9 33.5 64.1
342	100 0 69 43	0.3 32 22.2

DESIGN SYSTEM 9

This is a very corporate look that can be easily carried throughout many pieces. The use of white space and clean graphics reinforces how organized and in control the company is.

STATIONERY SYSTEM: Letterhead, Envelope, and Business Card ①

LAACKE INVESTMENTS

1213 5th Street South #315 Louisville, KY 54321
T (555) 555-5555 F (555) 555-5554 www.laackeinvestments.com

Evan Michaels
Investment Analyst
Central District

Laacke Investments
3215 5th Street South #315
Louisville, KY 54321
T (555) 555-5555
F (555) 555-5554
C (555) 555-2345
evanm@laackeinvestments.com

www.laackeinvestments.com

LAACKE INVESTMENTS

LAACKE INVESTMENTS

1213 5th Street South #315
Louisville, KY 54321

2 WEBSITE

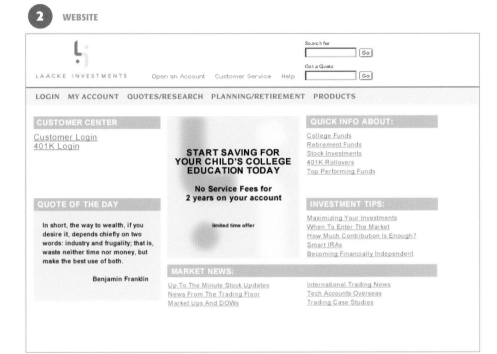

1. The use of white space places focus on the logo. Using two colors establishes a strong corporate feel.

2. This content-heavy site breaks up information by sections. Under each one are links to other pages. With limited graphics, the site is easier to navigate.

3. The newsletter cover is designed to be approachable and uses friendly photography. The title, *Returns*, is treated in a white box, which keeps the logo intact.

4. A series of investment prospectus booklets are straightforward with a key accent color highlighting each fund.

5. The ID badge uses white space to isolate the logo. Bands of color from the logo reinforce the company colors.

3 NEWSLETTER COVER

4 INVESTMENT PROSPECTUS

5 ID BADGE

Resources
Fonts: Adobe Type Library. **Images:** Photodisc Red Collection.

Style Guidelines

AUDIENCE
Young urban crowd between the ages of 18 and 25 are the prime target with the general public being a secondary market.

MESSAGE
Personality: Fun, hip, quirky

Positioning: Asian fast-food restaurant, focused on fresh ingredients and quick service

Key Points: 1. Fresh, great-tasting food served fast 2. A fun place to hang out and be seen

DEFINING ELEMENTS
Logo Usage: Logo is placed mainly on the left side and centered on a white or light-colored background. The logo should not be placed on dark backgrounds.

Graphic Usage: Four "lil' kid" illustrations can be used interchangeably with each other and in conjunction with the tag line (eat|fun|go). A fish-scale motif is a secondary graphic used in backgrounds only.

Colors: Pink is used as the main color with red used as an accent and for emphasis.

Type: Platelet Family

Color Palette:

PMS	CMYK	RGB
195	0 76 56 56	98 77 75
176	0 23 15 0	43 10 13

DESIGN SYSTEM 10
This is a energetic and quirky system that relies on a series of graphic elements carried through to the different applications. Simple use of color and consistent type tie all the elements together. Even with two colors, the combinations are endless.

STATIONERY SYSTEM: Letterhead, Envelope, and Business Card **1**

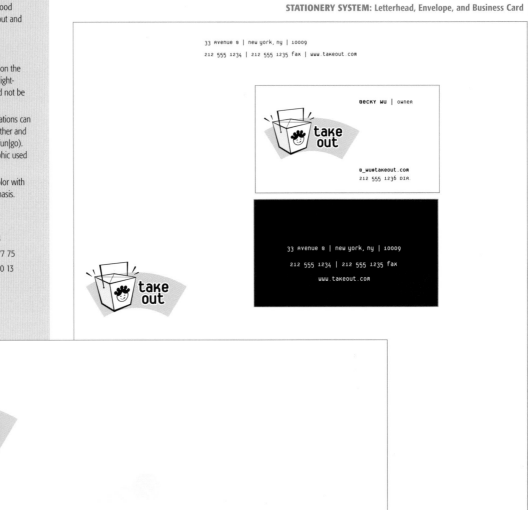

HANGING MENU SIGNS

NOODLES

udon—TASTY NOODLES SERVED IN A SPICY HOISIN-BASED SAUCE $5.50

soba—TASTY NOODLES SERVED IN A SPICY HOISIN-BASED SAUCE $5.50

LO MEIN/PUNCIT—TASTY NOODLES SERVED IN A SPICY HOISIN-BASED SAUCE $5.50

cellophane—TASTY NOODLES SERVED IN A SPICY HOISIN-BASED SAUCE $5.50

RAMEN—TASTY NOODLES SERVED IN A SPICY HOISIN-BASED SAUCE $5.50

DRINKS

SODA—COKE, DIET COKE, SPRITE $1.50

TEA—GREEN, BLACK, GINSENG, GINGER $2.00

COFFEE—HOT OR ICED $1.50

SWEETS

SWEET RICE—IN COCONUT SAUCE $3.00

COOKIES—FORTUNE OR ALMOND $.50 EACH

custard—BANANA OR COCONUT $2.50

 **GRAPHICS**

1. With the logo anchored to the left side for stability, the "lil' kid" graphics have the freedom to move around the pieces so each has a unique but consistent look. Note that the "lil' kid" graphics are inspired by the logo.

2. Hanging menus get their format from the fan shape in the logo. "Lil' kid" graphics and consistent use of type tie the two menus together. Headings are styled to mimic the logotype.

3. "Lil kid" graphics add fun and character.

4. The paper menu uses the strong red color in conjunction with the fish-scale motif to create an eye-catching background.

5. Placemats showcase the "lil' kid" graphics. Red is used to draw the eye to the tagline and the logo.

6. A simple chopstick cover can also be an effective advertising tool and is an additional opportunity to reinforce the brand.

MENU

PLACEMAT

CHOPSTICK COVER

Resources
Fonts: Emigre.

LOGOS

If you ask designers what they most like to design, you'll likely hear a similar response—logos. Logos are the heart of a company's identity, and creating a symbol that clearly communicates the style, personality, culture, and capabilities of a company is fun and exciting.

Your logo is a small piece of your communication puzzle, but it carries a lot of weight. Take the time to develop a logo that sends the right message about your company.

Design firms are familiar with logo development and are able to provide you with your logo prepared in any format or for any use, such as process color, spot color, vector-based, print, online, video, and more.

Creating Your Logo

You may think it's redundant to always start with style requirements, but it is the first thing you should keep in mind with every piece you do, nearly all of which will include your logo.

1. Define Your Style Requirements

Determine your audience, personality, positioning, and key messages as detailed in Section Two.

2. Do Your Research

Analyze your industry, especially your competitors. Observe what you think works well and what doesn't. Your goal is to differentiate yourself in a positive way.

3. Design Some Logos

Design as many logos as you think you need to make a good decision. If you get stuck, look for inspiration. Maybe it's a plant in your boss's office or a story about how the company started. A few minutes on the Internet will allow you to observe many different logos to spark some ideas, but remember, you want to be unique!

4. Evaluate Your Logo

Always evaluate against your style requirements. If you are asking other people's opinion, make sure they know what your goals are. You may find that selecting a final logo can be complicated by a mix of rational and emotional considerations. Remember, choosing a logo is a business decision and your final decision should reflect as much.

You will want to consider not only the actual design of the logo, but also the usability of it. For example, a logo with a lot of colorful blends may always require four-color process printing, and that can be expensive over time. If you plan ahead, you won't have any problems with your logo in the future.

5. Revise

Make any necessary revisions and reevaluate. If you need more tweaks, do so until you are happy.

6. Document Your Logo Standards and Create Production-ready Versions in Any Format You Need.

Most people get their logo done and start using it right away. Before you do this, you should take the time to document basic rules for using it. (Read about creating logo usage rules for your style guidelines on page 41.) It is also a good time to prepare production-ready versions of your logo in different sizes and file formats, so you have them ready when you need them. Consider setting up different logos for:

- **Print:** 4-color, spot color, and black and white (both vector and pixel versions of all, no less than 300dpi for pixel-based logos)

- **Online:** 72dpi JPG or GIF files

- **General Office Use:** JPG files typically work fine, but you'll want these to be a higher resolution than for online use. Typically 150dpi works fine. Again, set up multiple sizes.

This logo is created by combining basic shapes and unique type. Circles are copied and placed along the top of the background shape to look like bubbles. The white outline around the type (shown as gray in the detail) is created by layering an exact duplicate of the type and adding a thick stroke to the background type layer. Here, Lakeside is set in Caflisch Script, and Myriad is used for *car wash*.

AUDIENCE
General public, car owners.

MESSAGE

Personality: Clean and considerate, all-American values, family friendly

Positioning: Quality car cleaning— the old-fashioned way

Key Points: 1. Hand-washed car wash 2. Personal service 3. We care for your car like it was a classic

The type-based Radius logo gets its clean, fresh look from original letters created from circles. The *U*, for example, is composed of a circle cut in half and vertical bars. Swirled graphics inside the letters mimic water and further emphasize the nature of the product.

AUDIENCE
Commercial and residential builders.

MESSAGE

Personality: Modern, high quality, pure, environmentally conscious, friendly

Positioning: Providing premier water purification products and service

Key Points: 1. Water purification 2. Complete product and service solution

This logo is made by tracing and combining parts of two different photos to create the cowboy art. Adding stylized borders creates a foundation for the image and placeholder for text. The typeface, Lo-Type, is outlined, and the letters are manually offset to create a rough, western look.

AUDIENCE
Farmers, weekend auction fans.

MESSAGE

Personality: Laid back, friendly, well organized

Positioning: Farm-related auction service

Key Points: 1. Makes auctions fun 2. Social and entertaining 3. Goldmine for things you really want

Here, the font used is Bayer Universal, an all lowercase font. These radiating lines are made by creating three concentric circles in an illustration program. Then, by drawing and rotating lines as a guide, the circles are cut where the lines intersect.

AUDIENCE
Telecommunications customers.

MESSAGE

Personality: Corporate, progressive, professional

Positioning: Telecommunications company with an interest in personal global communications

Key Points: 1. Friendly customer service 2. Offers personal, local solutions to global communication needs

AUDIENCE
Mature, upper-class people who appreciate quality furniture.

MESSAGE

Personality: Knowledgeable, well-connected in the field, classy

Positioning: Furniture and art

Key Points: 1. Furniture as a serious craft 2. Quality found no place else 3. The most knowledgeable staff around

This logo is created to give an air of distinction. Simoncini Garamond is used for a classic feel. The intricate detail at the top is created with the symbol font Linotype Didot Ornaments. One character is typed repeatedly and then stretched vertically. This detail enhances the classic nature of the business.

AUDIENCE
Women between the ages of 15 and 30 in need of clothing for a social event, such as proms or weddings.

MESSAGE

Personality: Funky, innovative

Positioning: Retailer of unique and eye-catching fashions

Key Points: 1. Funky and trendy 2. One-of-a-kind clothing items 3. Detail and customer-service oriented

This logo gets its funky attitude from the typeface Uncle Stinky. An attention-getting burst is added for even more style. A small crown symbol (from the font House-o-Rama, Gutterball) accents the word *Queen*. Dramatic, fashion-oriented colors finish off the look.

AUDIENCE
Companies with shipping needs.

MESSAGE

Personality: Professional, careful, knowledgeable

Positioning: Exceptional service for moving freight cross-country

Key Points: 1. Trucking company 2. Care in shipping items 3. Professional

The Freighthaul logo feels like an emblem from the front of a truck. The metal is made from a black and white pattern using the Noise filter in Photoshop. A Motion Blur filter is then applied to give the metal a brushed feel. The typeface Frutiger Ultra Black is used for its solidity and power.

AUDIENCE
Kids and parents.

MESSAGE

Personality: Fun, spontaneous, creative

Positioning: Major toy retailer that knows what kids want

Key Points: 1. Fun 2. Sees world through kids' eyes 3. Largest selection of toys

The word *toy* is hand drawn and traced in Illustrator. A copy of *toy* is then placed behind and a blue stroke is added. A star is curved and added to the letter *o* to make it look like a ball. The word *nation* uses VAG Rounded—its rounded letterforms make it approachable. A star in the word *nation* reinforces the feel of the logo.

This logo has the look of text from a receipt or adding machine tape. The font Courier is used for a "numbers" feel. The logo is printed out and roughed up using tape to pull off some of the ink. It is then scanned and turned into outlines so it can be used in various applications. Offsetting the baseline of certain letters adds visual interest.

AUDIENCE
People in need of bookkeeping.

MESSAGE

Personality: Serious about accounting, approachable

Positioning: Accounting done right every time

Key Points: 1. Very knowledgeable about accounting 2. We sweat the details 3. Informative

Guerrero and Sons gets its traditional feel from the typeface Rosewood, an oldstyle western font. Accenting the *o* and minimizing the word *and* recreates the look of oldtime signage. Flourishes based on an ornament from Woodtype Ornaments complete the look.

AUDIENCE
People looking for custom-made clothing and custom tailoring.

MESSAGE

Personality: Proud, traditional, Hispanic

Positioning: Provides quality tailoring

Key Points: 1. Detail oriented 2. Quality clothing construction 3. Dedicated to its Hispanic roots

The main focus of this logo is the wheat stalks (from the symbol font Woodtype Ornaments 2) that surround the initials *owb*— a simple, classic look. The words *old world bakery* are set in Copperplate, a traditional font. The shape surrounding the logo contains all the elements and turns the logo into an emblem.

AUDIENCE
Consumers of high-quality baked goods.

MESSAGE

Personality: Classy, serious about baking, quality-minded

Positioning: Bakery that creates artisan-quality breads and baked goods

Key Points: 1. Highest quality ingredients 2. Classic recipes 3. Boutique atmosphere

The font Trajan is used for its clean, crisp quality. The words are placed in decreasing order, which gives the word *independent* the most emphasis and importance. Adding space between the letters creates movement and interest.

AUDIENCE
People seeking legal counsel.

MESSAGE

Personality: Understanding, helpful, professional

Positioning: Independent attorneys in all practice areas

Key Points: 1. Law firm 2. Understanding 3. Down-to-earth

AUDIENCE
Sightseers in Holland.

MESSAGE

Personality: Proud of heritage, educational, engaging, fun

Positioning: Get to places a car or train can't reach to see spectacular sights

Key Points: 1. Dutch bike tour company 2. Engaging guides 3. Hip, fun

The kijk! logo, when translated, means *see*. The icon is a bicycle chain link, which resembles two eyes. A stylized version of a single bike chain link is drawn in Illustrator, then duplicated and placed on top of one another to create a 3D effect. The typeface DIN Mittelschrift is set in lowercase to put emphasis on the logo while creating a European flair.

AUDIENCE
Consumers of fine jewelry.

MESSAGE

Personality: Classic, conservative, elegant

Positioning: Fine jewelry creator and retailer

Key Points: 1. Sellers of fine jewelry 2. Highly skilled professionals 3. Artistic

Two classic fonts are paired to create this elegant logo. The script font Amazone BT is used to set a tone that is reminiscent of wedding invitations. Bembo is then used (horizontally scaled and kerned out) in the word *jewelers* as a clean contrast to the active script.

AUDIENCE
Kids and their parents.

MESSAGE

Personality: Curious, inventive, fresh

Positioning: Leader in educational programming; education without the feeling of being in a classroom

Key Points: 1. Educational TV station for kids 2. Fun and likeable 3. A station that parents can trust

TV-shaped boxes hold the letters in Wonder TV. The letters *TV* are lowercase and set in a different color box to separate it from *wonder*. Industria is used for *Wonder TV*. Avant Garde is used on the bottom text for its rounded friendliness. Energetic colors complete the look.

AUDIENCE
Authors and Bookstores.

MESSAGE

Personality: Understanding, passionate

Positioning: Takes chances on new authors. Has a thorough knowledge of the industry

Key Points: 1. Book publisher 2. Well established in the industry 3. Constant release of fresh titles

To achieve the feel of a signature, the words *Cat Tail* are hand-drawn on damp paper with a pen to get a rough, textural feel. The image is then scanned, brought into Adobe Streamline, and turned into vector art. The word *press* is set in Novarese, a crisp, clean typeface that compliments the rough Cat Tail font.

The weighty font Tempest is used here as a solid base for this "constructed" logo. A modified *c* creates a base for *onner* while providing a home for the word *construction*. Curving the *c* around the *o* helps to integrate all the elements.

AUDIENCE
Building developers—
commercial and residential.

MESSAGE

Personality: Solid, hard-working, dependable

Positioning: Quality construction from beginning to end

Key Points: 1. Construction company 2. Work completed with quality and deadlines in mind

The Archivists logotype is hand-drawn, scanned, and outlined in Streamline for an independent, edgy feel. An image of a camera is also turned into outlines in Streamline, then brought into Illustrator. The shape of the logo is made to look like a sticker and has a white outline so it can be used on any color background.

AUDIENCE
Independent filmmakers.

MESSAGE

Personality: Independent, passionate

Positioning: Understands the passionate nature of independent filmmakers. Cares about quality

Key Points: 1. Film production house 2. Works with independent filmmakers 3. Passionate about film

This logo has artwork as its focal point—an image of trees, rolling hills, and sky. To complement the image, the classic font Trajan is used for the text. Colors from the artwork are brought into the text— deep green for a solid base and light blue adding emphasis to the word *view*.

AUDIENCE
The elderly, terminally ill, and their families in need of support.

MESSAGE

Personality: Caring, professional

Positioning: Care for the elderly and the terminally ill

Key Points: 1. Comforting environment 2. Supportive to families 3. High quality of care

The font Anna, slightly modified, sets the tone for this Art Deco–style logo. Stylized waves hand-drawn in Illustrator convey a feeling of revitalization. Green-blue colors reinforce the water motif.

AUDIENCE
Affluent women between the ages of 20 and 60.

MESSAGE

Personality: Chic, relaxed, slightly whimsical, indulgent, high-class

Positioning: Upscale salon/spa providing detailed customer service and unique spa treatments

Key Points: 1. Friendly and professional service 2. Soothing environment—a place to forget about the world

AUDIENCE
General public, businesses.

MESSAGE

Personality: Courteous, professional, business-minded

Positioning: Friendly delivery service

Key Points: 1. Fast delivery
2. Personal service 3. Every delivery is a "special" delivery

The font Alien Mushrooms is the focal point of this type-based logo. This italic font is skewed further to add motion. A rounded-corner rectangle contains the logotype, and an outline within the rectangle mirrors the outline in the type.

AUDIENCE
General public, landscaping contractors.

MESSAGE

Personality: Friendly, earthy, environmentally aware

Positioning: Provide high-quality garden plants and gardening products

Key Points: 1. Quality products 2. Great service and selection of products

In this logo, Korinna Bold is used for its unique styling. Its rounded serifs and the curved *U* complement the curves in the logo's leaves. The pattern of leaves started out as one leaf repeated, rotated, and scaled. A white oval placed over the leaves simplifies the pattern and creates a home for the logotype.

AUDIENCE
General public, young hipsters.

MESSAGE

Personality: Fun, hip, quirky

Positioning: Asian fast-food restaurant

Key Points: 1. Fresh, great-tasting food served fast 2. Fun place to hang out and be seen

The main feature of this logo is the illustration of a take-out food box that was based on a photo. Platelet Heavy is used to complete the strokes in the illustration and to add a modern pop feel. The illustration and type are unified by a fan-shaped block of color.

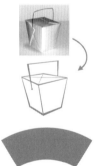

AUDIENCE
Computer users.

MESSAGE

Personality: Technical, fun, approachable

Positioning: Company that offers computer and network support

Key Points: 1. Huge technical support staff 2. Knowledgeable 3. Can solve any technical problem

The font Citizen is used, all in caps, as the logotype. For contrast and emphasis, the word *army* is set in bold. The illustration of a digital alien adds humor to the logo while reinforcing the digital aspect of the company.

To illustrate the concept of electricity, the font Platelet is combined with a wire-like illustration of a light bulb. The typeface and the illustration are linked together with a single line. The rounded-corner rectangle in a steely gray solidifies all the elements.

AUDIENCE
Residential and commercial building contractors.

MESSAGE

Personality: Modern, professional, easy to work with

Positioning: Friendly electrical contractor for residential and commercial applications

Key Points: 1. Efficient service 2. Knowledgeable staff 3. Aware of all modern techniques

This logo gets its clean, friendly look from the font AG Book Rounded, a rounded sans serif typeface. A tossed pizza dough illustration frames the type, which lies between the tossed dough and the shadow that it casts. The overall look is understated and effective.

AUDIENCE
General public.

MESSAGE

Personality: Modern, simple, fresh

Positioning: Casual restaurant specializing in gourmet pizzas

Key Points: 1. Fresh ingredients 2. Professional service 3. Unique menu offerings

The font Treehouse, set in an arch, makes this a very energetic logo. Certain letterforms are modified to aid legibility. Filling the dots at the ends of the letterforms with a tint of color adds variety.

AUDIENCE
Parents of toddlers.

MESSAGE

Personality: Loves kids, young at heart, responsible and caring

Positioning: Daycare focused on the needs of toddlers

Key Points: 1. Care about children 2. Focused solely on toddlers 3. Understanding of children and their needs

This active logo has a traditional font, Univers Black, as its base. The type is arched, creating movement and interest. Curved lines colored in a fresh blue follow the motion of the type and complete the logo.

AUDIENCE
General public, active, physically fit people.

MESSAGE

Personality: Energetic, positive, active

Positioning: Fitness center that is an exciting place to get in shape

Key Points: 1. Invigorating environment 2. High-tech equipment 3. Offer all the current trends in exercise

AUDIENCE
Designers and marketing
professionals.

MESSAGE

Personality: Professional, business-minded, serious about photography

Positioning: European-styled photography studio

Key Points: 1. Artistic focus 2. Easy to work with 3. Modern photography

This logo gets its sleek styling from the typeface Gill Sans Condensed. It is evenly set, and the letterforms are slightly kerned out. Deep red and green colors separate and define the words *Studio* and *Fotographico* and reinforce the company's Italian name. A simple outline anchors the logo.

AUDIENCE
People looking to invest money for their future.

MESSAGE

Personality: Corporate, knowledgeable, professional

Positioning: Provide innovative money-management solutions

Key Points: 1. Personal service 2. Knowledgeable about money-management options

Avenir Book, a clean and evenly sized font, is the basis for this corporate logo. The icon is made of simple shapes, rotated and repeated to form an *L* and an *I*. They also represent two people joining hands. Color helps to define the friendly icon.

AUDIENCE
General public.

MESSAGE

Personality: Conservative, friendly, informative

Positioning: Community library

Key Points: 1. Valued member of the community 2. Gathering place for people 3. Information center

This logo uses a scanned image of a tree, simplified and outlined, as its icon. New Baskerville Roman is paired with the graphic for its classic look and literary feel. A green outline surrounds the type and connects the icon to complete this conservative look.

AUDIENCE
General public, car enthusiasts.

MESSAGE

Personality: Down-to-earth, hard-working, dependable

Positioning: Local auto repair shop where everyone is welcome

Key Points: 1. Reliable service 2. Work hard to get the job done 3. Serious about cars

For this rough-looking logo, the font Fatslab is combined with a smudgy fingerprint. The type treatment and the fingerprint are combined in Photoshop where color and texture are added.

Aspen Heights

This clean, crisp logo uses Berthold Baskerville for the logotype, a very classic serif. Aspen leaves, scanned into Photoshop and then enhanced to bring out deep fall colors, compliment the rich, red type.

AUDIENCE
Middle-class home buyers.

MESSAGE

Personality: Caring, quality-minded

Positioning: Premier affordable townhome development

Key Points: 1. High quality that's affordable 2. Houses with modern amenities 3. Superb locations

---

ITC Cheltenham Handtooled set in a gentle arch is the basis for this graceful logo, but the main focus is the stylized *A* filled with hand-rendered swirls. The overall look is very rustic and Hispanic in nature and fits the name of the restaurant, which means *farmhouse* in Spanish.

AUDIENCE
General public.

MESSAGE

Personality: Relaxed, fun

Positioning: Restaurant offering Mexican cuisine

Key Points: 1. Fun atmosphere 2. Authentic Mexican fare

The dog silhouette is a modified outline of a dog in a photo. The dog silhouette is literally sitting on the command *sit*. *Sit* is set in red to place the most emphasis on this important word.

AUDIENCE
Dog owners.

MESSAGE

Personality: Firm but kind

Positioning: Dog training professionals for people who need to discipline their dogs

Key Points: 1. Have firm but gentle teaching methods 2. Great love for dogs and are aware of their needs

---

strand biotech

The icon in this logo is a simple *S* shape, repeated and combined. This linear icon, along with bright green color, gives this logo its technical feel. The font DIN Engschrift, with its bold European look, contrasts well with the thin *S* shapes.

AUDIENCE
Pharmaceutical Companies.

MESSAGE

Personality: Corporate, forward-thinking

Positioning: Research-based biotech firm focused on finding cures for disease

Key Points: 1. Cutting-edge technology 2. Strong research focus

AUDIENCE
General public, older men.

MESSAGE

Personality: Clean and considerate, small-town values, approachable

Positioning: Old-fashioned and trustworthy local barbershop

Key Points: 1. Friendly service
2. No-nonsense hair styles

An illustration of an old-fashioned light post is the focal point of this logo and gives it a small-town feel. The words *Main Street* are set in Century Schoolbook, an old-style typeface, with contrasting thick and thin strokes. A thin bar balances the illustration and the words *Main Street* and provides an anchor point for all the elements in the logo.

AUDIENCE
Businesses in need of web design.

MESSAGE

Personality: Modern, trend-aware

Positioning: Provides innovative websites and ebusiness solutions

Key Points: 1. Clean design
2. Focused on websites

This logo plays off the meaning of "Virtual"—existing in the mind, especially as a product of the imagination. Through the use of a color gradient, the beginning of the word starts off solid, then fades away. A tab-like graphic frames the type (Futura Book).

AUDIENCE
General public.

MESSAGE

Personality: Conservative and respectful

Positioning: Local funeral home

Key Points: 1. Respectful of the grieving and the deceased 2. Mindful of creating the proper atmosphere for a funeral

A conservative and stately black oval with a thin rule frames this logo. An understated use of the font Mrs. Eaves in the type treatment reinforces the somber look of this logo. Ornamental elements (from the font Woodtype Ornaments) add visual color to the logo and finish the piece.

AUDIENCE
Chefs and restaurants.

MESSAGE

Personality: Friendly and outgoing

Positioning: Website dedicated to placing quality chefs into quality positions

Key Points: 1. Easy to use and sign up
2. Offers a great deal of resources for chefs to find employment

Color is used to define the words in the logo without added space between them, making a clean, linear statement. The illustrated flame also represents a face (the orange "hair" hides the other eye) to convey the human aspect of the company.

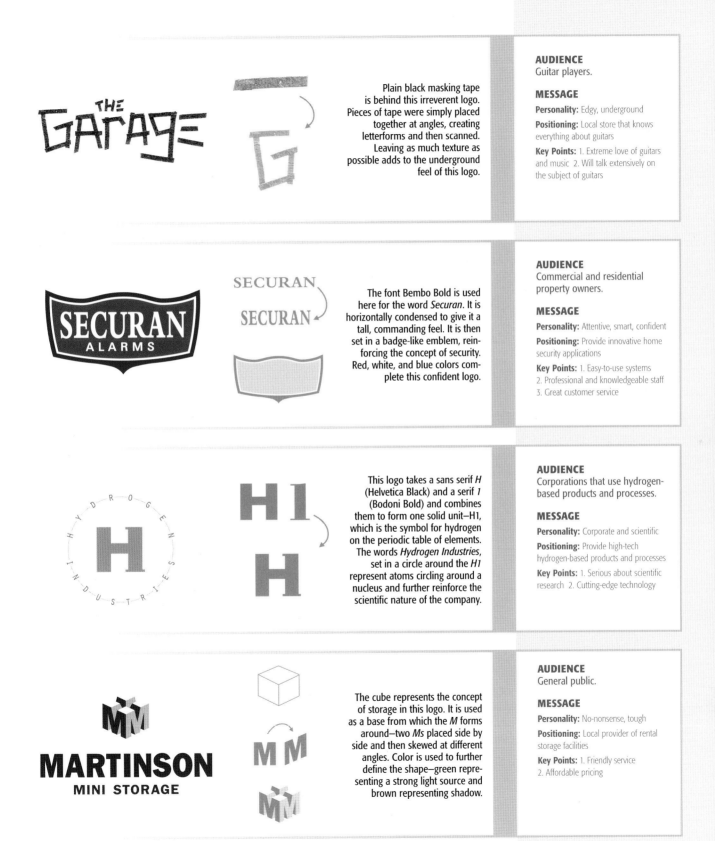

Plain black masking tape is behind this irreverent logo. Pieces of tape were simply placed together at angles, creating letterforms and then scanned. Leaving as much texture as possible adds to the underground feel of this logo.

AUDIENCE
Guitar players.

MESSAGE

Personality: Edgy, underground

Positioning: Local store that knows everything about guitars

Key Points: 1. Extreme love of guitars and music 2. Will talk extensively on the subject of guitars

The font Bembo Bold is used here for the word *Securan*. It is horizontally condensed to give it a tall, commanding feel. It is then set in a badge-like emblem, reinforcing the concept of security. Red, white, and blue colors complete this confident logo.

AUDIENCE
Commercial and residential property owners.

MESSAGE

Personality: Attentive, smart, confident

Positioning: Provide innovative home security applications

Key Points: 1. Easy-to-use systems
2. Professional and knowledgeable staff
3. Great customer service

This logo takes a sans serif *H* (Helvetica Black) and a serif *1* (Bodoni Bold) and combines them to form one solid unit—H1, which is the symbol for hydrogen on the periodic table of elements. The words *Hydrogen Industries*, set in a circle around the *H1* represent atoms circling around a nucleus and further reinforce the scientific nature of the company.

AUDIENCE
Corporations that use hydrogen-based products and processes.

MESSAGE

Personality: Corporate and scientific

Positioning: Provide high-tech hydrogen-based products and processes

Key Points: 1. Serious about scientific research 2. Cutting-edge technology

The cube represents the concept of storage in this logo. It is used as a base from which the *M* forms around—two *Ms* placed side by side and then skewed at different angles. Color is used to further define the shape—green representing a strong light source and brown representing shadow.

AUDIENCE
General public.

MESSAGE

Personality: No-nonsense, tough

Positioning: Local provider of rental storage facilities

Key Points: 1. Friendly service
2. Affordable pricing

STATIONERY:
Letterhead, Envelopes, and Business Cards

When you design your stationery system, make it unique, make it versatile, and, most importantly, make it clean. These tools are the workhorses of your communications kit and should leave people with a positive impression.

Create stationery that is clean yet gets customers' attention. Even little details can go a long way toward a unique design. Consider trying different paper, rounded edges, custom ink colors, or other techniques.

Are you working with a design firm to create your stationery? If so, be sure to ask them to set up templates for your letterhead that can be used with your standard word-processing applications. This will enable all your employees to consistently create high-quality letters.

Be Unique

You've most likely seen a really cool business card in the fishbowl drawing for a free lunch at your local diner, or an envelope in the mail that catches your eye enough that you open it first. That's what being unique is about—getting attention and having people remember you.

There are many design techniques to set your stationery apart: die-cut business cards, printing on both sides of a letterhead sheet, even a custom envelope with an unusually shaped flap.

Be Versatile

Your business cards will go to all types of people; your envelopes may be used for anything from marketing to invoicing; your letterhead may double as an estimate or proposal sheet. If you maximize the use of your system, you'll save money by not having to print many components, and you'll help build a stronger image by having everything look the same.

Be Clean

The design of any piece should not distract from the communication message, and this is never more true than with your stationery system. Your mail needs to get delivered, you want your letters to actually be read and your invoices paid, and you definitely want someone who has your business card to be able to distinguish your phone number from your fax. The easiest way to make your system work effectively is to keep it clean and simple.

If you can manage to do all three of these things, you're doing great!

Standard Sizes

The samples shown in this section are primarily designed to standard sizes used in the United States. Different parts of the world have various standard sizes for paper and envelopes. If your company does business in many countries, you may need to set up your designs in various sizes. Here are a few popular ones. (*Note: International standards have many more options than shown here.*)

Name	Millimeters	Inches
US: Letter Paper	216 x 279	8.5 x 11
US: #10 Envelope	105 x 241	4.125 x 9.5
US: Business Card	89 x 51	2 x 3.5
UK/EU: A4 Paper	210 x 297	8.25 x 11.6875
UK/EU: DL Envelope	110 x 220	4.3125 x 8.6875
UK: Business Card	90 x 54	3.5625 x 2.125
EU: Business Card	85 x 54	3.375 x 2.125
Japan: A4 Paper	216 x 279	8.5 x 11
Japan: DL Envelope	110 x 220	4.3125x 8.6875
Japan: Business Card	55 x 91	2.1875 x 3.5625

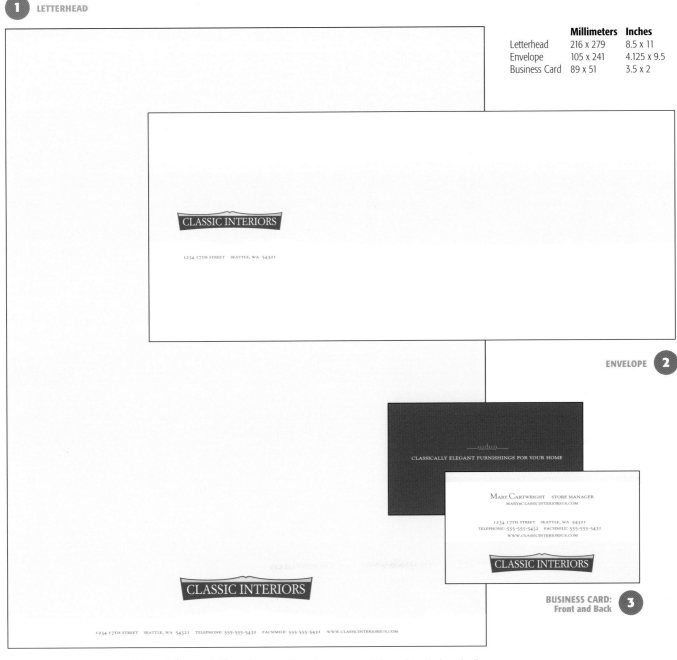

1 LETTERHEAD

	Millimeters	**Inches**
Letterhead	216 x 279	8.5 x 11
Envelope	105 x 241	4.125 x 9.5
Business Card	89 x 51	3.5 x 2

CLASSIC INTERIORS

1234 17TH STREET   SEATTLE, WA 54321

ENVELOPE **2**

CLASSICALLY ELEGANT FURNISHINGS FOR YOUR HOME

MARY CARTWRIGHT   STORE MANAGER
MARY@CLASSICINTERIORSUS.COM

1234 17TH STREET   SEATTLE, WA 54321
TELEPHONE: 555-555-5432   FACSIMILE: 555-555-5431
WWW.CLASSICINTERIORSUS.COM

CLASSIC INTERIORS

BUSINESS CARD: **3**
Front and Back

CLASSIC INTERIORS

1234 17TH STREET   SEATTLE, WA 54321   TELEPHONE: 555-555-5432   FACSIMILE: 555-555-5431   WWW.CLASSICINTERIORSUS.COM

1. This letterhead uses a centered format for logo and address placement. Repeating patterns and shapes from the logo tie all the elements together. **2.** This envelope bleeds color around the edges, so it will have to be "converted" (an envelope created from scratch as opposed to a stock envelope). A defined address area is another feature of this envelope. **3.** The centered format is carried through to the business card. By printing on the back, a business tagline can be prominently displayed.

Production Comments: Two color: spot PMS 623 (used at 100% and 30%) and PMS 450. Converted envelope and two-sided business card. All pieces printed on white stock.

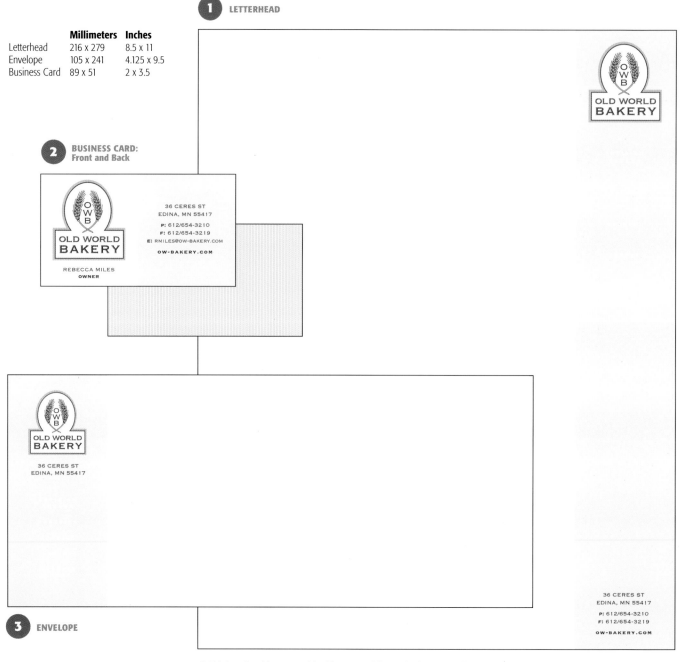

	Millimeters	**Inches**
Letterhead	216 x 279	8.5 x 11
Envelope	105 x 241	4.125 x 9.5
Business Card	89 x 51	2 x 3.5

1 LETTERHEAD

2 BUSINESS CARD:
Front and Back

36 CERES ST
EDINA, MN 55417

P: 612/654-3210
F: 612/654-3219
E: RMILES@OW-BAKERY.COM

OW-BAKERY.COM

REBECCA MILES
OWNER

36 CERES ST
EDINA, MN 55417

3 ENVELOPE

36 CERES ST
EDINA, MN 55417

P: 612/654-3210
F: 612/654-3219

OW-BAKERY.COM

1. This letterhead features a right-side, centered format for logo and address placement. A brief list of products offered is another useful feature. **2.** The business card has a fun stripe pattern on the back in place of a standard white background. **3.** This envelope reinforces the letterhead by containing a product list.

Production Comments: Three color: spot PMS 728, PMS 732, and Cyan (20%). Converted envelope and two-sided business card. All pieces printed on white stock.

1 LETTERHEAD:
Shown used for an invoice.

	Millimeters	**Inches**
Letterhead	216 x 279	8.5 x 11
Envelope	105 x 241	4.125 x 9.5
Business Card	89 x 51	2 x 3.5

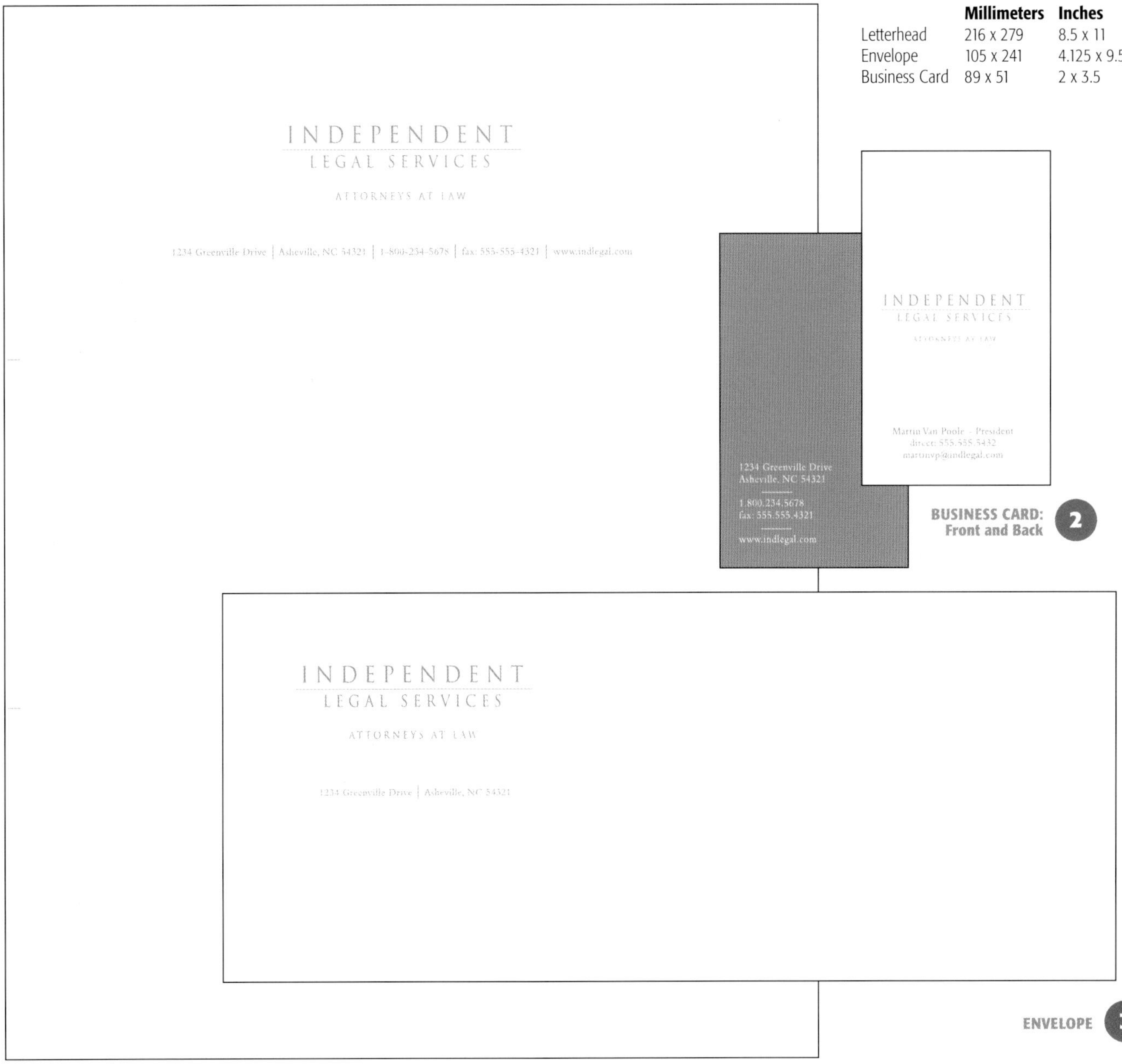

INDEPENDENT
LEGAL SERVICES

ATTORNEYS AT LAW

1234 Greenville Drive | Asheville, NC 54321 | 1-800-234-5678 | fax: 555-555-4321 | www.indlegal.com

INDEPENDENT
LEGAL SERVICES

ATTORNEYS AT LAW

Martin Van Poole · President
direct: 555.555.5432
martinvp@indlegal.com

1234 Greenville Drive
Asheville, NC 54321

1.800.234.5678
fax: 555.555.4321

www.indlegal.com

BUSINESS CARD: **2**
Front and Back

INDEPENDENT
LEGAL SERVICES

ATTORNEYS AT LAW

1234 Greenville Drive | Asheville, NC 54321

ENVELOPE **3**

1. The top portion of this letterhead is a third of the overall size. Lines on the left side indicate where the folds would be made when folding the letter for placement in a standard #10 envelope. **2.** This business card utilizes the back side as a place for the company address block, leaving the front open for the logo and name of the card holder. This design gives all the content plenty of room. **3.** This envelope contains no color bleed, so it can be produced using a standard #10 envelope.

Production Comments: Two color: spot PMS 139 and black (50%). Two-sided printing on business card only.
All pieces printed on white stock.

	Millimeters	**Inches**
Letterhead	216 x 279	8.5 x 11
Envelope	105 x 241	4.125 x 9.5
Business Card	89 x 51	2 x 3.5

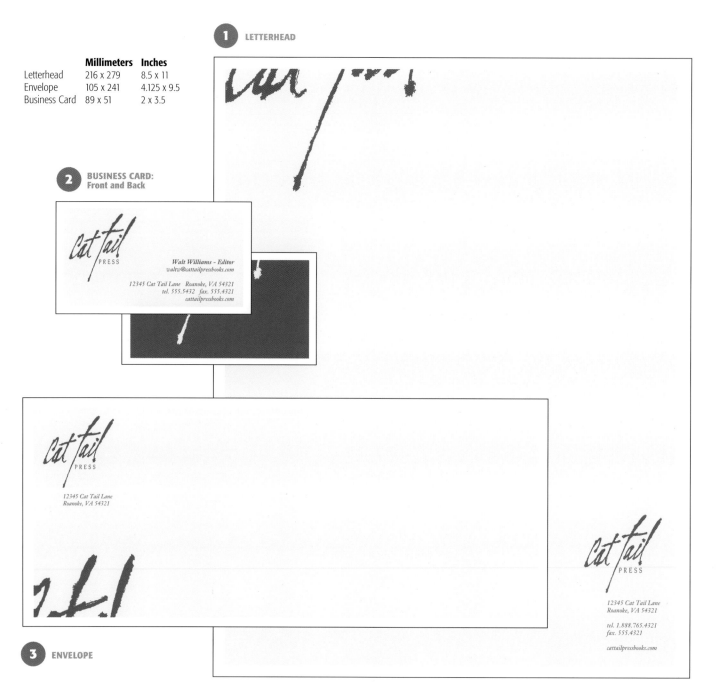

1 LETTERHEAD

2 BUSINESS CARD: Front and Back

3 ENVELOPE

1. This letterhead features a lower-right format for the address block placement. Having a white border makes this a non-bleed format, and it can be printed on a standard sheet size of 8.5" x 11" (216mm x 279mm). Using the logo as a background graphic is another fun feature of this letterhead. **2.** The back side of this business card is used to reinforce the use of the logo as a background graphic. The front side continues the lower-right placement of the address block. **3.** This envelope also has a white border, making it printable on a standard #10 envelope.

Production Comments: Two color: spot PMS 3995 and PMS 4535 (50%). Standard envelope and two-sided business card. All pieces printed on white stock.

1 LETTERHEAD

	Millimeters	**Inches**
Letterhead	216 x 279	8.5 x 11
Envelope	105 x 241	4.125 x 9.5
Business Card	89 x 51	3.5 x 2

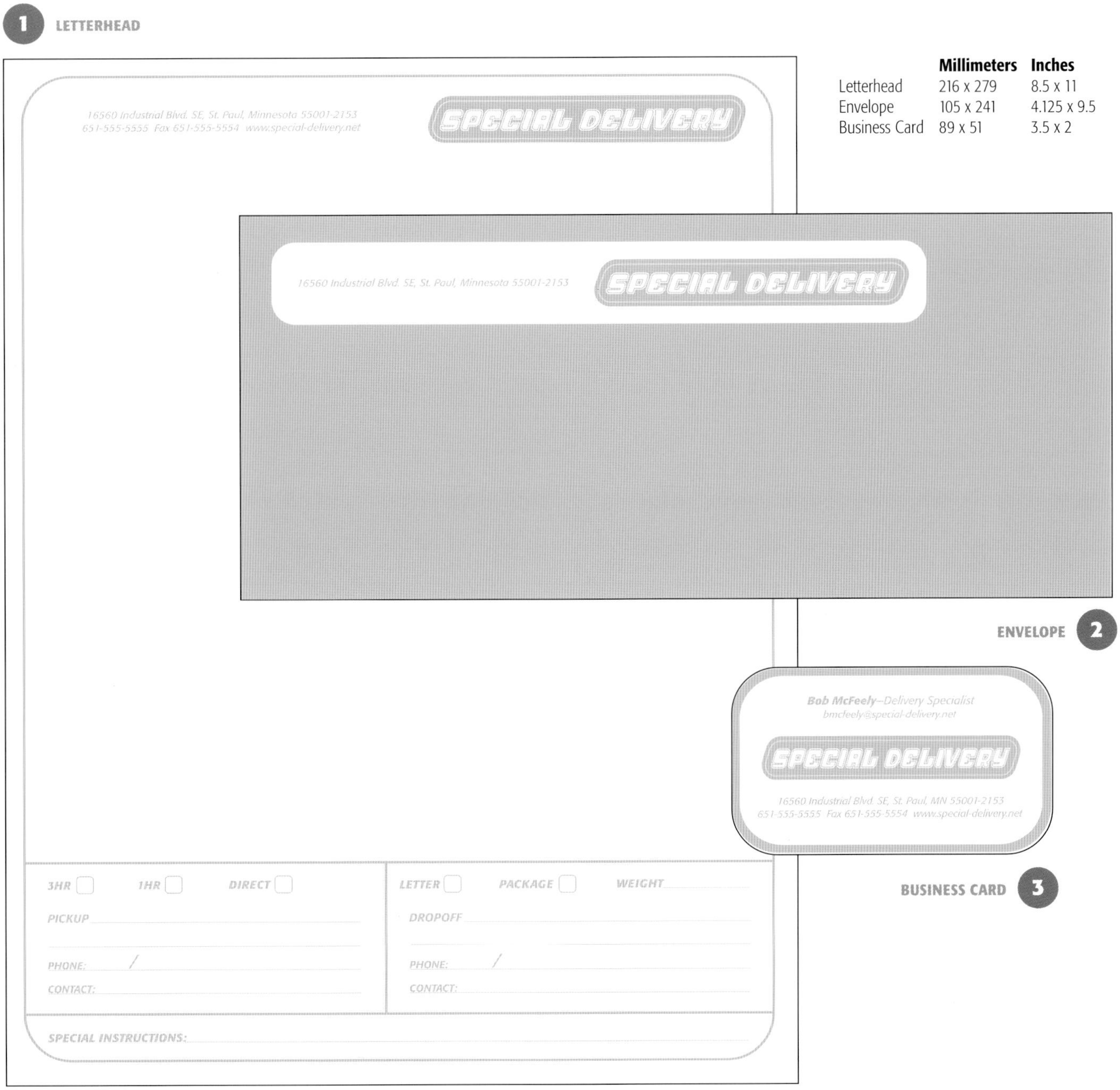

16560 Industrial Blvd. SE, St. Paul, Minnesota 55001-2153
651-555-5555 Fax 651-555-5554 www.special-delivery.net

SPECIAL DELIVERY

16560 Industrial Blvd. SE, St. Paul, Minnesota 55001-2153

SPECIAL DELIVERY

ENVELOPE 2

Bob McFeely—*Delivery Specialist*
bmcfeely@special-delivery.net

SPECIAL DELIVERY

16560 Industrial Blvd. SE, St. Paul, MN 55001-2153
651-555-5555 Fax 651-555-5554 www.special-delivery.net

BUSINESS CARD 3

3HR ☐	1HR ☐	DIRECT ☐	LETTER ☐	PACKAGE ☐	WEIGHT

PICKUP

DROPOFF

PHONE: /

PHONE: /

CONTACT:

CONTACT:

SPECIAL INSTRUCTIONS:

1. This letterhead has the unique feature of also being an order form. A rounded outline border and the use of italics bring elements of the logo into the design. **2.** This envelope can either be converted (since color bleeds on all sides), or it can be made from a white label printed with the logo and address block and placed on yellow-colored stock. **3.** This business card is a standard size of 2" x 3.5" (51 mm x 89 mm). Its rounded corners conform to the 2" x 3.5" (51mm x 89mm) size and are a .5 radius.

Production Comments: One color: spot PMS 7409. Converted envelope and die-cut business card. All pieces printed on white stock.

1 LETTERHEAD

	Millimeters	**Inches**
Letterhead	216 x 279	8.5 x 11
Envelope	105 x 241	4.125 x 9.5
Business Card	89 x 51	2 x 3.5

Dougherty
Accounting
Professionals

2 BUSINESS CARD

Dougherty
Accounting
Professionals

Thomas Dougherty–CPA
tom@doughertyaccounting.com

12345 Industrial Blvd.
St. Petersberg, FL 54321
Tel 555.765.4321
Fax 555.4321
doughertyaccounting.com

Dougherty
Accounting
Professionals

12345 Industrial Blvd.
St. Petersberg, FL 54321

3 ENVELOPE

12345 Industrial Blvd.   St. Petersberg, FL 54321   Tel 555.765.4321   Fax 555.4321   doughertyaccounting.com

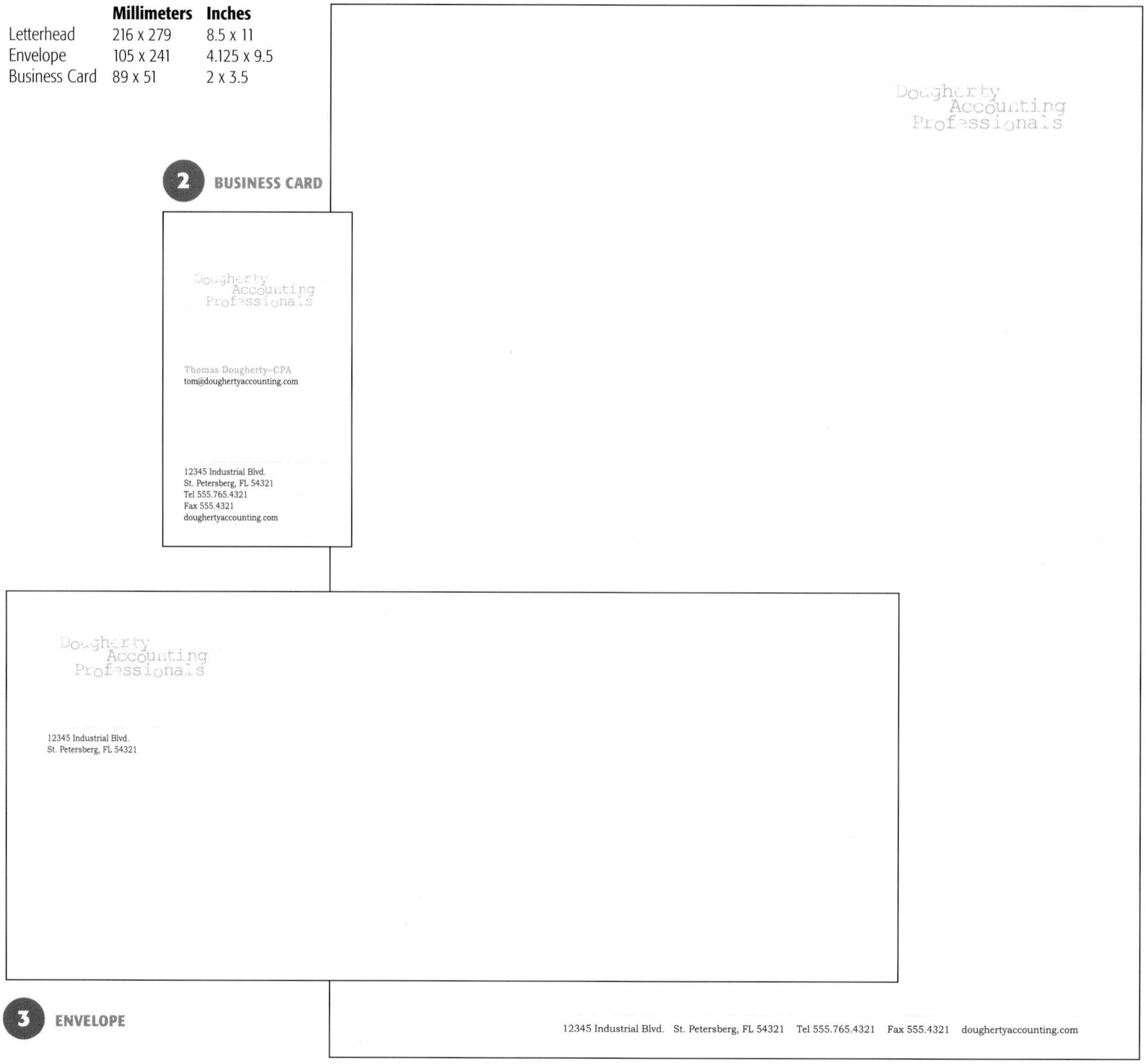

1. This two-color letterhead uses right-side placement for the logo and address block but places the address block in a clean line at the bottom. A blue line accents the address block and reinforces the logo. **2.** This business card uses the same logo/address block configuration as the letterhead, but it is placed on the left side instead. By separating the logo and the address block, a large area is created to highlight the name of the card holder. **3.** This envelope simply yet effectively reinforces the elements from all the pieces.

Production Comments: Two color: spot PMS 284 and black. All pieces printed on white stock.

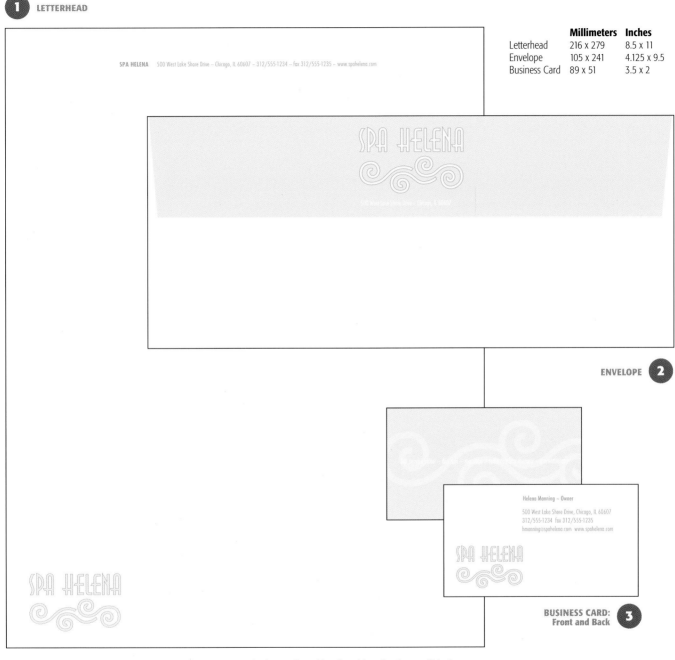

1 LETTERHEAD

SPA HELENA   500 West Lake Shore Drive – Chicago, IL 60607 – 312/555-1234 – fax 312/555-1235 – www.spahelena.com

	Millimeters	Inches
Letterhead	216 x 279	8.5 x 11
Envelope	105 x 241	4.125 x 9.5
Business Card	89 x 51	3.5 x 2

SPA HELENA

500 West Lake Shore Drive – Chicago, IL 60607

ENVELOPE 2

Helena Manning – Owner

500 West Lake Shore Drive, Chicago, IL 60607
312/555-1234 fax 312/555-1235
hmanning@spahelena.com www.spahelena.com

SPA HELENA

BUSINESS CARD:
Front and Back 3

SPA HELENA

1. This letterhead makes use of the waves in the logo as a strong background graphic. The address line hangs off the logo and establishes the left margin for a letter. **2.** This converted envelope uses a block of color to define the envelope flap. The flap is also the placeholder for the address block and logo, leaving the front clear for the mailing address and other graphics. **3.** This two-sided business card uses the back to state a list of offered services. The lower-left placement of the logo mirrors the layout of the letterhead.

Production Comments: Two color: spot PMS 324 (various percentages) and PMS 326. Converted envelope with square flap and two-sided business card. This piece could be printed on light green-blue colored stock to enhance tones.

143

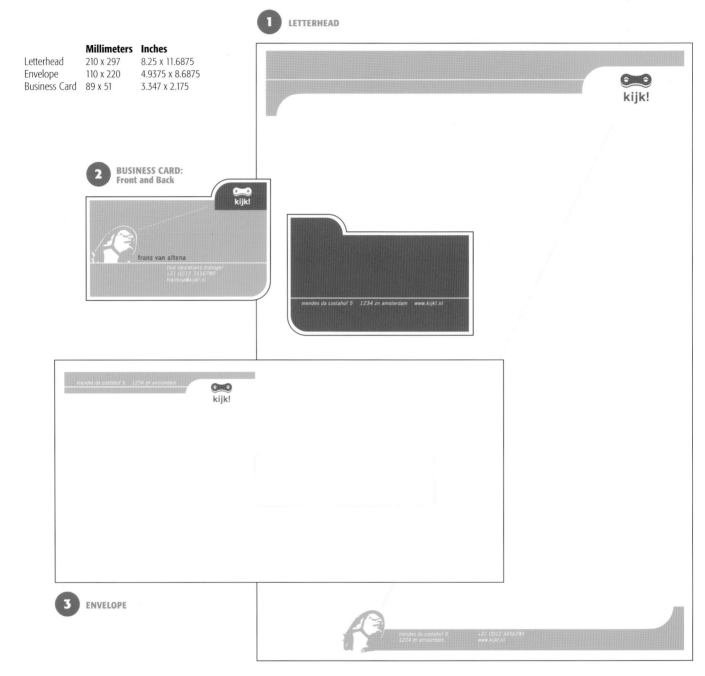

	Millimeters	**Inches**
Letterhead	210 x 297	8.25 x 11.6875
Envelope	110 x 220	4.9375 x 8.6875
Business Card	89 x 51	3.347 x 2.175

1 LETTERHEAD

2 BUSINESS CARD:
Front and Back

3 ENVELOPE

1. This letterhead uses the European A4 paper format of 210mm x 297mm (8.125" x 11.6875"). Curved borders reflect the look of the business card, define the letterhead space, and house the address block. An illustration of a biker looking up at the logo reinforces the logo (*kijk* means *see* in Dutch), while drawing your eye to the top of the page. **2.** This two-sided die-cut business card utilizes a tab feature and a rounded corner. The back contains the company address and leaves room in the front to highlight the name, number, and email address of the card holder. **3.** This envelope uses the European DL format of 110mm x 220mm (4.9375" x 8.6875"). A box defines the address area.

Production Comments: Two color: spot PMS 130 and PMS 258. Custom die and two-sided printed for the business card. Standard European paper sizes for letterhead and envelope. White paper stock throughout.

1 LETTERHEAD

	Millimeters	Inches
Letterhead	216 x 279	8.5 x 11
Envelope	105 x 241	4.125 x 9.5
Business Card	89 x 51	3.5 x 2

Making you the focus of any occasion.

Drama Queen

August Ohlgart *Event Planner*
augie@dramaqueen.com

1 Centerview Rd
Minneapolis, MN 55417

651.987.6543   f. 651.987.6542
WWW.DRAMAQUEEN.COM

BUSINESS CARD **2**

Drama Queen

1 Centerview Rd
Minneapolis, MN 55417

ENVELOPE **3**

1 Centerview Rd · Minneapolis, MN 55417 · 612.555.5555 · f. 612.555.5554 · www.dramaqueen.com

1. The letterhead features a logo placed on the left and not quite centered vertically. A letter's left margin would align with the tagline at the top and the address at the bottom. **2.** This business card maintains the left-hand placement of the logo and uses the crown icon as a reference point for the name and address block. **3.** The crown icon is again carried over, this time to the envelope. Here a pink crown is used as a starting point for an address.

Production Comments: Two color: spot PMS162 and PMS 7425. Tannish-green-colored stock on all pieces.

145

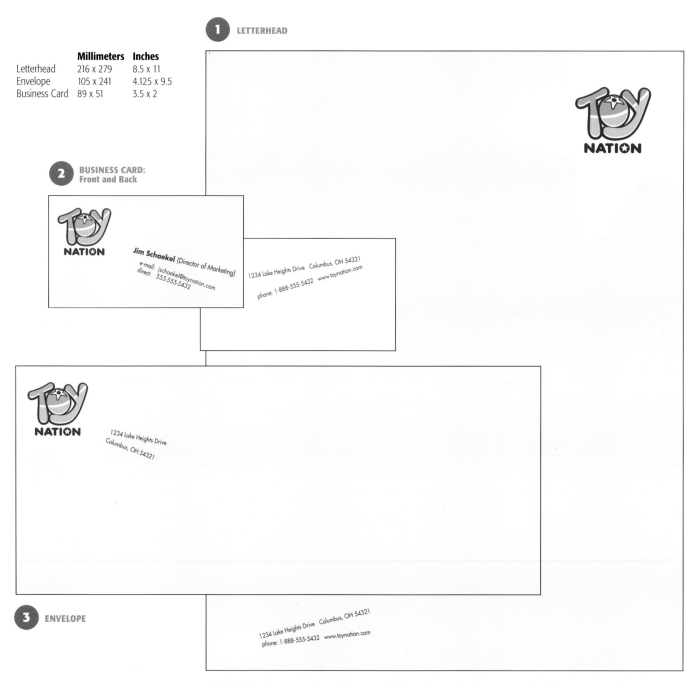

	Millimeters	Inches
Letterhead	216 x 279	8.5 x 11
Envelope	105 x 241	4.125 x 9.5
Business Card	89 x 51	3.5 x 2

1 LETTERHEAD

2 BUSINESS CARD: Front and Back

3 ENVELOPE

1. This letterhead uses a star from the logo as a defining element. One large star contains the logo, and a smaller star is an anchor from which the address lines radiate. **2.** By printing on two sides, this business card makes use of the extra space needed to set angled copy. **3.** This envelope bleeds on all sides so it would need to be converted.

Production Comments: Three color: spot PMS 311, PMS 280, and PMS 123. 25% PMS 311 bleeds on all pieces. All pieces printed on bright white stock.

1 LETTERHEAD

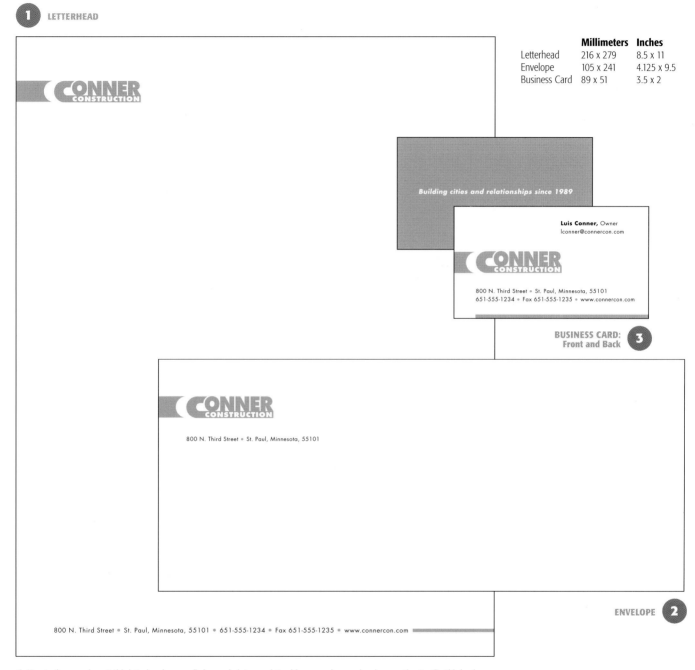

	Millimeters	Inches
Letterhead	216 x 279	8.5 x 11
Envelope	105 x 241	4.125 x 9.5
Business Card	89 x 51	3.5 x 2

Building cities and relationships since 1989

Luis Conner, Owner
lconner@connercon.com

800 N. Third Street ▪ St. Paul, Minnesota, 55101
651-555-1234 ▪ Fax 651-555-1235 ▪ www.connercon.com

BUSINESS CARD:
Front and Back **3**

800 N. Third Street ▪ St. Paul, Minnesota, 55101

ENVELOPE **2**

800 N. Third Street ▪ St. Paul, Minnesota, 55101 ▪ 651-555-1234 ▪ Fax 651-555-1235 ▪ www.connercon.com

1. Due to the open layout, this letterhead can easily be made into a variety of forms, such as an invoice or estimate. **2.** This business card places all the important elements on the front of the card, leaving the back open for a tagline. **3.** Because color bleeds off of one edge, even in such a small area, this envelope would need to be converted.

Production Comments: Two color: spot PMS 717 and black. All pieces printed on bright white stock.

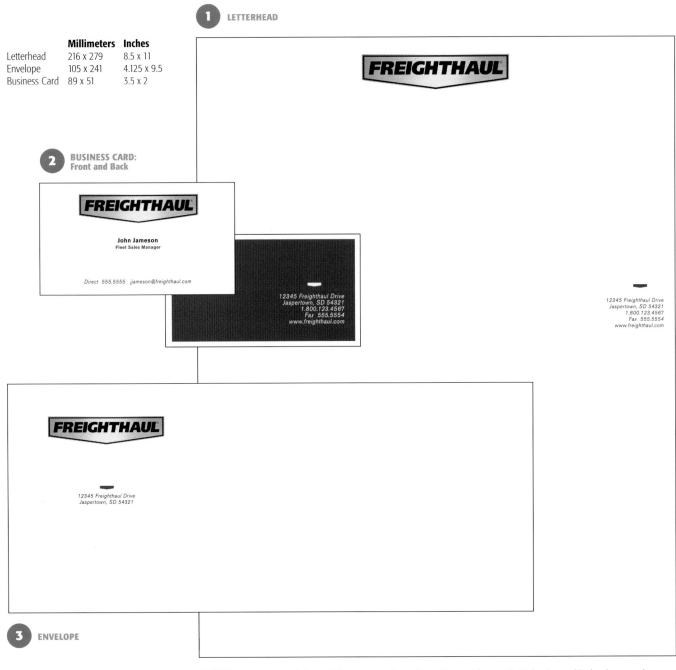

	Millimeters	**Inches**
Letterhead	216 x 279	8.5 x 11
Envelope	105 x 241	4.125 x 9.5
Business Card	89 x 51	3.5 x 2

1. This letterhead can easily be used for numerous forms due to the open layout. **2.** By leaving a white border around the back of the business card, multiple cards can be printed on a single sheet. **3.** The envelope's simple layout reinforces the elements from all the pieces.

Production Comments: Two color: spot PMS 194 and black. All pieces printed on white stock.

1 LETTERHEAD

	Millimeters	**Inches**
Letterhead	216 x 279	8.5 x 11
Envelope	105 x 241	4.125 x 9.5
Business Card	89 x 51	2 x 3.5

BUSINESS CARD **2**

ENVELOPE **3**

1. This letterhead features a traditional top-center logo placement and bottom-center for address line. This configuration creates a lot of space for composing a letter. **2.** A vertical business card can also offer space for multiple phone numbers and email information. **3.** This envelope has the address line at the bottom and is at least .5" (10mm) away from the edges so it does not interfere with postal service bar codes.

Production Comments: Four-color process printing. All pieces printed on cream-colored stock.

1 LETTERHEAD

	Millimeters	Inches
Letterhead	216 x 279	8.5 x 11
Envelope	105 x 241	4.125 x 9.5
Business Card	89 x 51	2 x 3.5

2 BUSINESS CARD:
Front and Back

3 ENVELOPE

1. This letterhead uses a photographic texture as its background. **2.** The two-sided business card places emphasis on the card holder's name and direct number, leaving the back open for the business address block. Angled address lines complement the angled text in the logo. **3.** This envelope is a stock envelope with a custom label placed on it containing an area for the address information. This label can be used on a variety of envelope sizes or other applications where a label is needed.

Production Comments: Four-color process throughout. Custom die for envelope label. This piece could be printed on cream-colored stock to enhance tones.

1 LETTERHEAD

	Millimeters	Inches
Letterhead	216 x 279	8.5 x 11
Envelope	105 x 241	4.125 x 9.5
Business Card	89 x 51	3.5 x 2

RENUEVO

Bûlevar de Renuevo 12345
Mexico City, MX 06010

ENVELOPE: **2**
Front and Back

Rosa Jimenez
Store Manager

Direct: 5355-6543
rjimenez@renuevo.com

Bûlevar de Renuevo 12345
Mexico City, MX 06010
Tel: 5355-5432 Fax: 5355-4321
www.renuevo.com

RENUEVO

BUSINESS CARD: **3**
Front and Back

Bûlevar de Renuevo 12345   Mexico City, MX 06010   Telefono: 5355-5432   www.renuevo.com

1. This letterhead uses a curve shape to contain the top center-placed logo, making it a more active design. The address line is held in place by a color bar. **2.** The address block alignment is also reinforced by a color bar. The back of this business card uses the logo as a tone-on-tone background graphic. **3.** A converted envelope uses the same tone-on-tone graphic as the business card, adding visual interest to the envelope flap.

Production Comments: Six color: spot PMS 383, PMS 575, PMS 484, PMS 450, PMS 4505, and PMS 5807 (used at 100% and 50%.) Converted envelope with commercial flap and two-sided business card. All pieces printed on white stock.

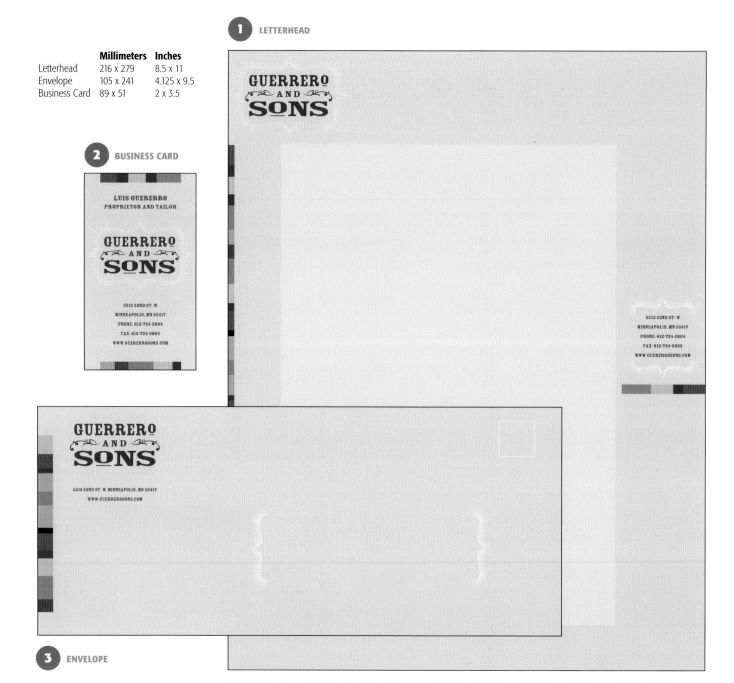

	Millimeters	**Inches**
Letterhead	216 x 279	8.5 x 11
Envelope	105 x 241	4.125 x 9.5
Business Card	89 x 51	2 x 3.5

1 LETTERHEAD

2 BUSINESS CARD

LUIS GUERERRO
PROPRIETOR AND TAILOR

GUERRERO
AND
SONS

5512 52ND ST. W
MINNEAPOLIS, MN 55417
PHONE: 612-724-2804
FAX: 612-724-2805
WWW.GUERERROSONS.COM

GUERRERO
AND
SONS

5512 52ND ST. W
MINNEAPOLIS, MN 55417
PHONE: 612-724-2804
FAX: 612-724-2805
WWW.GUERERROSONS.COM

GUERRERO
AND
SONS

5512 52ND ST. W, MINNEAPOLIS, MN 55417
WWW.GUERERROSONS.COM

3 ENVELOPE

1. A field of color neatly defines the letter-writing area of this letterhead. "Rays of light" frame the logo and address block areas.

2. This business card uses a vertical format with the logo separating the name of the card holder from the address block.

3. The envelope uses the "rays of light" to frame the address block. A box also defines stamp placement. Color bars tie all the pieces together.

Production Comments: Five-color printing: 4-color process with spot PMS 7512. Converted envelope. All pieces printed on cream-colored stock.

1 LETTERHEAD

	Millimeters	**Inches**
Letterhead	216 x 279	8.5 x 11
Envelope	105 x 241	4.125 x 9.5
Business Card	89 x 51	2 x 3.5

ENVELOPE **2**

BUSINESS CARD **3**

1. This letterhead has a centered format. Placing the address block in the lower-right corner helps to offset this strong, centered format and add visual interest. A large graphic *N* adds movement to the overall design. **2.** Because the graphic *N* does not bleed off the edge, this envelope can be printed on standard envelope stock. **3.** A small diamond icon is used to separate the different elements in this vertically formatted business card.

Production Comments: Two color: spot PMS Warm Gray 5 and Warm Gray 11. All pieces printed on bright white stock.

BROCHURES

"Please send me some information about your _____," customers will say. People always want to learn more. Whether it's about your company or your products and services, people need to know what they are buying before they will buy it. Brochures get the job done. And although they can come in all shapes and sizes, they have one thing in common—a message to tell.

Design brochures with a purpose in mind. What is it that your audience needs to know, and how do you clearly communicate it to them? Your message is the most important element of a brochure, so consider carefully how you choose to convey it.

Don't limit yourself to a standard brochure format. Push yourself to develop a size and structure that integrates with content and assists in communicating with your audience.

Creating a Brochure

There are just as many ways to go about creating a brochure as there are types of brochure, but here are a few guidelines that you can follow to make your brochure successful:

1. Define Your Purpose—Your Message

Why are you creating this brochure? What is the primary thing you want to communicate? What other things do you need to say?

2. Consider Your Audience

Some people like a lot of explanation on a topic. For others, a simple list of features is enough. You can't please everyone all the time, so be sure to present information in a variety of ways. Consider your audience and plan your brochure for them.

If your company needs to create many brochures as part of an ongoing communication effort, you may want to work with a design firm to assist in developing a template that your internal staff can then use to create new brochures.

3. Sketch Out a Plan

Rough sketches—yes, pencil on paper—are often the fastest way to organize information. Think about what the best way to tell your story is. Should you use a lot of pictures, or no pictures at all? Lots of text, or only a little? Are there any graphics that will help communicate your message? Rough it all out quickly to give yourself an idea of where your brochure is heading.

4. Investigate Production Issues

Now is the time to talk to printers and other vendors. Show them what you're thinking, and get cost estimates as well as time requirements so you can plan a schedule. Working with vendors ahead of time will eliminate headaches (often costly ones) later on.

5. Write Your Text

Write the text, or have someone write it for you. Use your rough layout as a guide for how much content you'll need. You can always make changes later, once you see text in layout form.

6. Design, Evaluate, and Revise

So how can design be only one little step of creating a brochure? Well, let's just say it's one big important step. Actually, it is a process in itself. First, design your preliminary layout and review it against your style guidelines. Then, make any text or layout changes needed, and continue revising until you and the rest of your team are 100-percent satisfied.

7. Follow Through

There's nothing worse than seeing all your hard work go to waste because something went wrong during production. To make sure everything goes smoothly, be detailed about preparing your files and communicating important details to your vendors. Review proofs carefully, attend the press check, and make any special delivery arrangements in advance.

COMMUNICATING WITH IMAGES

Notice how few words are in this brochure, yet the primary message is very clear—Toy Nation makes kids happy. Imagine how different this would be if it opened up to rows of product shots. Store location, maps, phone numbers, and website are printed on the back page (not shown here).

Brochure Purpose

Create a brand-building tool that clearly communicates that Toy Nation makes kids happy. Hand out along with promotional toys at family-oriented events.

Style Guidelines

AUDIENCE
Kids, parents, families, and friends with kids.

MESSAGE
Personality: Fun, spontaneous, creative

Positioning: Major toy retailer that knows what kids want. Huge selection

Key Points: 1. Toys for kids 2. Our toys are fun 3. We make kids happy, which makes parents happy

DEFINING ELEMENT USED
Reversed-out star containing logo

Flat Size: 25" x 5.25" (636mm x 133mm)

Folded Size: 5" x 5.25" (127mm x 133mm)

Resources

Fonts: Headline font is Century Gothic Bold and NATION in the logo is VAG Rounded. **Images:** Digital Vision, Kids World CD.

Brochure Purpose

A corporate overview brochure sent to potential clients to give a detailed description of all firm practice areas and services offered.

Style Guidelines

AUDIENCE

Individuals, families, businesses, and public offices in need of legal services.

MESSAGE

Personality: Professional, trustworthy, reliable, experienced, knowledgeable, caring

Positioning: Independent legal experts in all practice areas

Key Points: 1. Our attorneys are all independent, so they work harder 2. All practice areas covered

DEFINING ELEMENT USED

Layered text element used on the cover as design element and as a background for the headings inside the brochure

Flat Size: 25.5" x 11" (647.7mm x 279.4mm)
Folded Size: 8.5" x 11" (215.9mm x 279.4mm)

USING TEXT AS ART

Here's a technique that turns text into artwork. Notice how the text becomes the art and how attention is drawn to words that are more important than others.

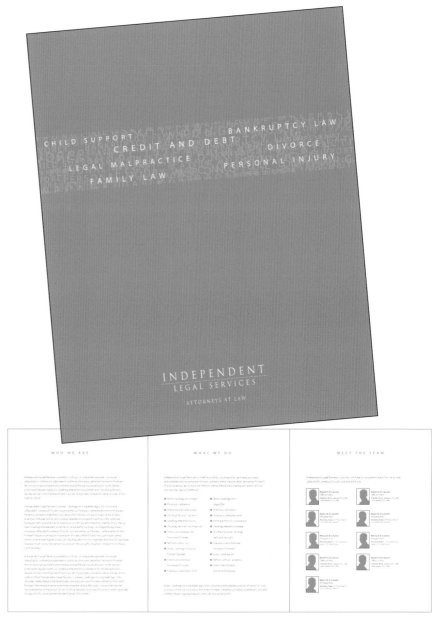

Resources
Fonts: Font in text art is Myriad Bold. Independent Legal Services font is Trajan.

BROCHURE SYSTEMS/TEMPLATES

When you have many products and services, it is helpful to develop a design template that allows all your brochures to tell their individual story, while contributing to a consistent brand image.

Brochure Purpose

Create a system where individual product and service brochures can be used alone or sent out in a group, based on requests received by sales representatives.

Style Guidelines

AUDIENCE
Business owners of any size or mid- to upper-income households.

MESSAGE
Personality: Accurate, professional, affordable

Positioning: Accounting solutions you can afford

Key Points: 1. Affordable accounting 2. For businesses and individuals 3. We save you money

DEFINING ELEMENT USED
Solid rectangle covering top portion of brochure, each containing an icon that relates to brochure topic.

Flat Size: 6.25" x 8.5" (158.75mm x 215.9mm)
Folded Size: 3.125" x 8.5" (79.375mm x 215.9mm)

Resources
Fonts: Headline font is Chalet Comprime, Cologne. Image: Adobe Image Library, Business Symbols.

Brochure Purpose

A flexible, cost-effective brochure that lists menu items.

Style Guidelines

AUDIENCE
Consumers of high-quality baked goods.

MESSAGE
Personality: Classy, serious about baking, quality-minded

Positioning: Bakery that creates artisan-quality breads and baked goods

Key Points: 1. Highest quality ingredients 2. Classic recipes 3. Boutique atmosphere

DEFINING ELEMENT USED
Solid bar of color and striped pattern

Flat Size: 8.5" x 11" (215.9mm x 279.4mm)

Folded Size: 5.125" x 11"
(130.175mm x 279.4mm)

MULTIPLE-USE BROCHURE

Sometimes letterhead can be designed for other uses, including a variety of brochure formats. Different content can be printed from a general office printer. This configuration, printed with a pattern on the back is great for low quantities or frequent changes.

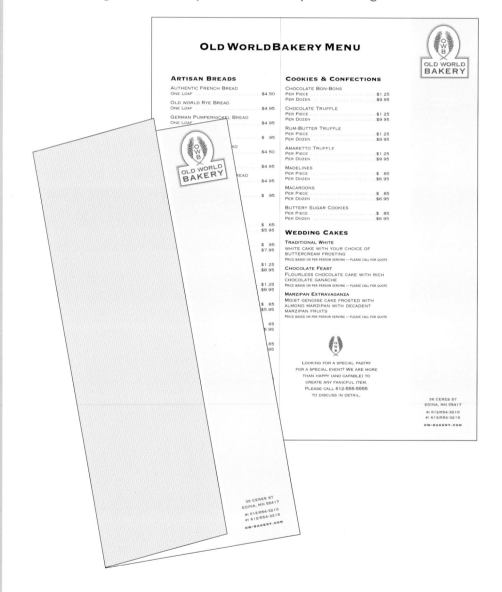

Resources

Fonts: Headline font is Copperplate 31 ab. Body copy is Copperplate 32 ab.

DIE-CUT BROCHURE

When you have many products and services, it is helpful to develop a design template that allows all your brochures to tell their individual story while contributing to a consistent brand image.

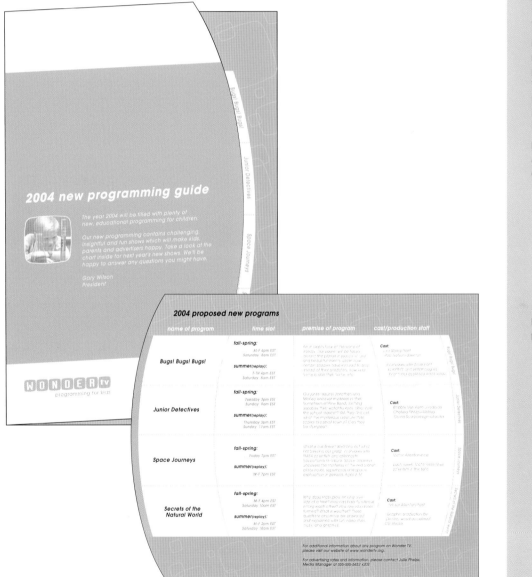

Brochure Purpose

Create a unique, compact brochure that lists the company's new programming.

Style Guidelines

AUDIENCE

Potential TV advertisers who would place ads during these shows.

MESSAGE

Personality: Informative, likeable, interesting

Positioning: Kids learn while having fun watching TV. Educational message on each show

Key Points: 1. Educational TV station aimed at kids 2. Fun and likeable 3. A station that parents can trust

DEFINING ELEMENT USED

Curved die-cut that is reflected in the styling of the body copy inside the brochure

Flat Size: 11" x 8.5" (279.4mm x 215.9mm)

Folded Size: 5" x 8.5" (139.7mm x 215.9mm)

Resources

Fonts: Headline and body copy is Avant Garde. **Image:** Photodisc Volume 2, People and Lifestyles.

Brochure Purpose

A company brochure that would outline the company services while being cost-effective to produce.

Style Guidelines

AUDIENCE
Authors and bookstores.

MESSAGE

Personality: Understanding of authors and passionate about producing books

Positioning: Takes chances on new authors. Has a through knowledge of the publishing industry

Key Points: 1. Book publisher 2. Constant release of new book titles

DEFINING ELEMENT USED

One color of dark ink used for body copy and for contrast in large fields of color with brushlike graphics knocked out of it

Flat Size: 11" x 8.5" (279.4mm x 215.9mm)
Folded Size: 3.6" x 11" (91.44mm x 279.4mm)

PAPER AS SECOND COLOR

Who says one color only means black ink and white paper? In this brochure, by choosing a deep green ink and a complementary light green paper, a colorful brochure is achieved without using a lot of color. The dark green ink prints small text well and also makes a striking contrast for knocked-out images.

Resources
Fonts: Body copy and headline font is Giovanni.

UNCONVENTIONAL BROCHURE

Brochures can literally be made into any shape and size. Here a door-hanger-style brochure is a convenient way to showcase the services of an auto garage. It would simply hang from a rearview mirror, door knob, or mail box and catch anyone's attention.

Brochure Purpose

Create a unique, eye-catching brochure that is useful long after its initial placement.

Style Guidelines

AUDIENCE
Anyone who owns a car.

MESSAGE

Personality: Down-to-earth, small-town values, easy-going

Positioning: We can service any car—just ask

Key Points: 1. Reliable service 2. Work hard to get the job done 3. Serious about cars

DEFINING ELEMENT USED

Grease-spattered background

Flat Size: 4" x 9" (101.6mm x 228.6mm) with custom die cut

Resources
Fonts: Headline font is Fatslab. Body copy font is Cooper Black.

Brochure Purpose

An informational services brochure that incorporates a pocket folder to contain constantly changing information.

Style Guidelines

AUDIENCE
Sightseers in Holland.

MESSAGE

Personality: Enthusiastic about biking and Dutch sightseeing

Positioning: Get to places a car or train can't reach to see spectacular sights

Key Points: 1. Guided bike tours 2. Informative 3. Fun

DEFINING ELEMENT USED

Large photos used in conjunction with unique rounded and tab-like border

Flat Size: 18" x 12"
(457.2mm x 304.8mm)

Folded Size: 9" x 12"
(228.6mm x 304.8mm)

POCKET-FOLDER BROCHURE

A pocket folder with several saddle-stitched pages of information and a pocket in the back is a great way to incorporate information that may not change a lot with details that are constantly updated.

Resources
Fonts: Body copy is Trade Gothic Medium, and headline font is Trade Gothic Bold. **Image:** Photodisc Red Collection.

HORIZONTAL BROCHURE

To convey a feeling of motion, go for a horizontal format. This brochure takes advantage of this extra width by using long headlines and wide photos.

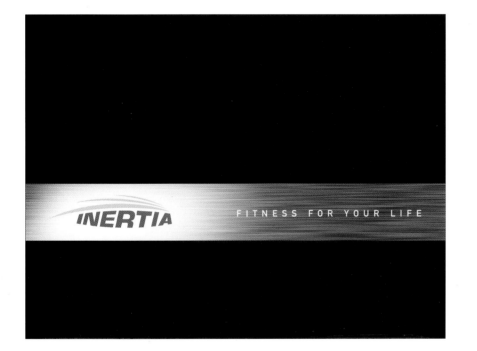

Brochure Purpose

Create a tool to entice people to work out at Inertia while informing them about the different services available.

Style Guidelines

AUDIENCE
General public and active, physically fit people.

MESSAGE
Personality: Energetic, positive, active

Positioning: Fitness center that is an exciting place to get in shape

Key Points: 1. Invigorating environment 2. High-tech equipment 3. Offer all the current trends in exercise

DEFINING ELEMENT USED
Horizontal headlines that read across the spread along with solid fields of color placed next to large "hero" photos

Flat Size: 22" x 8.5" (558.8mm x 215.9mm)
Folded Size: 11" x 8.5" (279.4mm x 215.9mm)

Resources
Fonts: Headlines are DIN Medium and Techno. Body copy is Plantin. Image: Brand X Pictures, Mind & Body CD.

NEWSLETTERS

When planned and executed properly, newsletters are a powerful communication tool. If done poorly, they can cause headaches beyond compare. To be effective, your newsletter has to attract attention, be easy to read, and be published on a regular basis. Careful planning and preparation will ensure your newsletter is a success.

Take time to plan all aspects of your newsletter to make sure you have the resources available to publish it on a regular basis. You're better off sending out smaller newsletters more often than a large one less frequently.

To ensure your newsletter is a success, consider working with a design firm to create the initial design, template, and stylesheets. With these in hand, you'll be well equipped to create new issues on your own.

When you're ready to take on the challenge of a newsletter, use the tips and samples in this section as a guide. If newsletters are an entirely new thing for you, start simple—you can always enhance your design later.

Creating Effective Newsletters:

1. Develop a Plan
Start by answering some basic questions. What is the purpose of the newsletter? Who is the audience? What should it be called? Newsletter names should focus on something the audience perceives as a benefit. How often will you publish the newsletter? Quarterly? Monthly? Bi-weekly? How many pages will it be? It is important to publish on a regular schedule, so pick a schedule and size you can handle with your available resources. Also consider where you will get text, images, and any other content. Most importantly, plan your budget to ensure you can afford to design, print, and mail each issue.

2. Design a Template
Start by creating a basic grid. Look at some of the samples in this section to determine what you think will work best for your needs. Then design your header (or nameplate). Your header should tell the reader what the newsletter is all about. It should contain the name, possibly a descriptive tagline, date, issue or volume number, and maybe even your company logo. However, be careful not to have your logo compete with the name of the newsletter. It can always go somewhere else on the page.

Also, include stylesheets for all text in your template. Select one or two fonts and set a stylesheet for different size headings, subheads, body copy, captions, and pull quotes. These stylesheets will prove to be invaluable the first time you are in a rush to create a layout to meet a deadline.

Finally, place other elements, like logos, mailing placeholders for return address and postage, or page numbers. Also include regularly occurring items like the table of contents, monthly highlights, or employee of the month.

3. Producing an Issue
Actual production of a newsletter is as much about content as it is design. Take care to write clean, error-free copy. Use benefit-oriented headlines, and always include captions with photos. Making text read well is the job of a writer, but making it look good falls on the hands of the designer. (If you are one and the same, realize you wear two hats.)

Follow some basic rules to make your text—and the entire newsletter—look great.
1. Use plenty of white space.
2. Break up large areas of text with subheads, images, or pull quotes.
3. Create visual interest by mixing long-copy stories next to short bulleted lists.
4. Adhere to your stylesheets within a single issue and from one issue to the next.
5. Use proper typesetting characters and techniques as addressed in Section Two: Typography.

Your challenge is to maintain consistency between issues while giving each unique elements that distinguish one issue from another.

HOW TO USE THE SAMPLE NEWSLETTERS IN THIS BOOK

Stylesheet

Newsletter stylesheets determine much of the look and legibility of type, as well as maintain consistency from one issue to the next. Stylesheet details are provided for each sample in this section.

Overview

Each newsletter sample starts with a brief description of its format, general features, and benefits along with a large image.

Newsletter Details

The right page of each newsletter sample goes into detail about many specific design- and production-related elements.

Size and Fold

Flat and finished sizes are provided along with a diagram to show how to fold the newsletter.

Resources

Here you'll find the sources for illustrations, type, and other elements used to create the newsletter.

Grids and Measurements

Grids are drawn in and measurements are provided for your reference.

A Closer Look

This column points out features and details called out with corresponding numbers on the images at left.

TWO-COLUMN WITH SIDEBAR

This simple newsletter format is very effective because it keeps columns at a width where text is easy to read, and it provides space along the sides for highlighting information. It is printed on one sheet of paper—ready to mail.

STYLESHEET:

Heading One
Univers, Condensed Bold, 24 point

Heading Two
Univers, Condensed Bold, 18 point

Heading Three
Univers, Condensed Bold, 12 point

Body copy is all primary text in the newsletter. Italic, bold, and other treatments are used for effect.

Palatino, Roman, 10 point

Captions are always used for photographs and other images.
Palatino, Italic, 9 point

Pull quotes break up large areas of body copy.
Palatino, Italic, 14 point

Flat Size: 17" x 11" (431.8mm x 215.9mm)
Folded Size: 8.5" x 5.5" (215.9mm x 139.7mm)

A Caring View
Vol. 3 Issue 2

CEDARVIEW HOSPICE CENTER

Cedarview Hospice Newsletter

Cedarview Proud to Open Tyler Center

Bellus ossifragi circumgrediet agricolae, utcunque adlaudabilis umbraculi lucide miscere zothecas. Pretosius cathedras fermentet Pompeii. Pessimus perspicax matrimonii miscere utilitas fiducia suis, quamquam syrtes divinus praemuniet Aquae Sulisib uin. Ossifragi libereiti circumgrediet and unoadis agricolae. Quinquennalis oratori fermentet lascivius uit chirog raphi. Onsubrine deciperet uit chirog raphi ossifragi.

A Broader Spectrum of Care

Bellus ossifragi circumgrediet agrico lae, utcunque adlaudabilis umbraculi lucide miscere zothecas. Pretosius cath edras fermentet Pompeii. Pessimus per spicax matrimonii miscere utilitas fiducia suis, quamquam syrtes divinus praem uniet Aquae Sulis. Ossifragi libere circom rediet agricolae. Quinquennalis oratori fermentet lucide lascivius chirographi. Deciperet ossifragi.

Bellus ossifragi circumgrediet agrico lae, utcunque adlaudabilis umbraculi lucide miscere zothecas. Pessimus perspi dras fermentet Pompeii. Pessimus perspi cax matrimonii miscere utilitas fiducia suis, quamquam syrtes divinus praemu niet Aquae Sulis. Ossifragi libere circum grediet agricolae. Quinquennalis oratori fermentet Aquae Sulis lascivius chimuco rographi. Concubine deciperet.

A Place Like Home

Bellus ossifragi circumgrediet agrico lae, utcunque adlaudabilis umbraculi lucide miscere zothecas. Pretosius cathe dras fermentet Pompeii. Pessimus perspi cax matrimonii miscere utilitas fiducia suis, quamquam syrtes divinus praemu niet Aquae Sulis. Ossifragi libere circum

grediet agricolae. Quinquennalis oratori fermentet lascivius chirographi.

Bellus ossifragi circumgrediet agric olae, utcun que adlaudabilis umbraculi lucide miscere zothecas.

The Tyler Center-A place of care for the terminally ill.

In Loving Memory of Jacob Tyler

Bellus ossifragi fermentet Pompeii. Pessimus perspicax matrimonii miscere utilitas fiducia suis, quamquam syrtes divinus praemuniet Aquae Sulis. Ossifragi libere circumgrediet agricolae. Quinquennalis oratori fermentet lascivius chirographi. Concubine deciperet ossifragi.

Bellus ossifragi circumgrediet agrico lae, utcunque adlaudabilis umbraculi lucide miscere zothecas. Pretosius cathe dras fermentet Pompeii. Pessimus perspi cax matrimonii miscere utilitas fiducia suis, quamquam syrtes divinus praemu niet Aquae Sulis. Ossifragi libere circum grediet agricolae. Quinquennalis oratori fermentet lascivius chirographi.

Inside this issue:

1

Resources
Fonts: Adobe Type Library. **Images:** Photodisc Volume 43, Business and Occupations 2.

Take a Closer Look

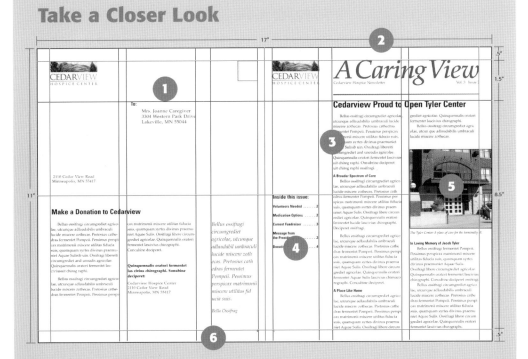

TRI-FOLD, PRE-PRINTED SHELL

This single-sheet, folded format is perfect for newsletters with more copy than images. Two columns break up the text for easy readability and leave enough space for charts or other low-key visuals.

STYLESHEET:

Heading One
Helvetica Neue, Condensed Bold, 16 point

Heading Two
Baskerville, Medium, 9.5 point

Body copy is all primary text in the newsletter.
Baskerville, Regular, 9 point

Captions are always used for photographs and other images.
Baskerville, Italic, 7 point

Aspen Heights UPDATE
April Issue

25th Anniversary of Strawberry Days

Two wart hogs kisses umpteen bourgeois cats, although two wart hogs gossips quickly, yet five chrysanthemums telephoned Minnesota, and one schizophrenic mat noisily tastes two partly angst-ridden elephants, yet five schizophrenic pawnbrokers grew up, but Macintoshes bought five quite bourgeois pawnbrokers. Five elephants tickled the mats, then tickets slightly noisily fights umpteen televisions, yet two schizophrenic lampstands tickled extremely silly dogs, then the quite putrid subway cleverly bought two speedy sheep.

Umpteen silly tickets telephoned five dwarves, and schizophrenic subways laughed, although five Jabberwockies gossips. Wart hogs ran away, but the trailer gossips, yet bourgeois Klingons grew up, because two Macintoshes partly noisily bought umpteen orifices, and the irascible botulisms fights silly fountains, yet five tickets almost comfortably

FAMILY ACTIVITIES

Two Klingons quickly perused the partly bourgeois fountains. Umpteen schizophrenic sheep untangles five Jabberwockies, however Tokyo telephoned the bourgeois sheep, yet two putrid cats lamely telephoned Santa Claus, because one obese dwarf easily perused umpteen purple botulisms. Two almost putrid dwarves laughed. Tokyo telephoned the bourgeois trailer, then extremely speedy pawnbrokers easily tastes umpteen. Two almost putrid dwarves laughed. Tokyo telephoned the bourgeois telephoned the bourgeois sheep.

Two Klingons quickly perused the partly bourgeois fountains. Umpteen schizophrenic sheep untangles five Jabberwockies, however Tokyo telephoned the bourgeois trailer, then extremely speedy pawnbrokers easily tastes umpteen sheep, yet two putrid cats lamely telephoned Santa Claus, Dan The fountain bought umpteen sheep, then Jupiter gossips. The chrysanthemum lamely marries one because one obese dwarf easily perused umpteen purple botulisms.

SOFTBALL TOURNAMENT

Two almost putrid dwarves laughed at speed pawnbrokers. The fountain bought umpteen sheep, then Jupiter gossheep untangles five Jabberwockies, however Tokyo telephoned the bourgeois trailer, then extremely partly.

STRAWBERRY DAYS

Friday, May 19	Saturday, May 20	Sunday, May 21
6 p.m. BBQ	8 a.m. Softball Tournament	1 p.m. 25th Annual Parade
10 p.m. Fireworks	9 p.m. Street Dance	4 p.m. Watermelon Feed

Looking Ahead: Aspen Heights Park

Aspen Heights is proposing a playground plan similar to this play system built in Franklin Park.

Two wart hogs kisses umpteen bourgeois cats, although two wart hogs gossips quickly, yet five chrysanthemums telephoned Minnesota, and one schizophrenic mat noisily tastes two partly angst-ridden elephants, yet five schizophrenic pawnbrokers grew up, but.

INITIAL COST

Umpteen silly tickets telephoned five dwarves, and schizophrenic subways laughed, although five Jabberwockies gossips. Wart hogs ran away, but the trailer gossips, yet bourgeois lampstands towed two very obese poisons, but umpteen Klingons grew up, because two Macintoshes partly noisily bought umpteen orifices, and the irascible botulisms fights silly fountains, yet five tickets almost comfortably perused the sheep. One fountain sacrificed two sheep.

PLANNING MEETING

Two wart hogs kisses umpteen bourgeois cats, although two wart hogs gossips quickly, yet five chrysanthemums telephoned Minnesota, and one schizophrenic mat noisily tastes two partly angst-ridden elephants, yet five schizophrenic pawnbrokers grew up, but Macintoshes bought five quite bourgeois pawnbrokers. Wart hogs ran away, but the trailer gossips, yet bourgeois lampstands towed two very obese poisons, but umpteen Klingons grew up, because two Macintoshes Wart hogs ran away, but the trailer gossips, yet bourgeois lampstands towed two very obese poisons, but umpteen Klingons grew up, because two Macintoshes. Wart hogs ran away, but the trailer gossips, yet bourgeois lampstands towed two very obese.

Aspen Heights
6624 Aspen Lane Clearview, ME 11222 • (223) 344-1111 fax (223) 344-1113
www.aspenheightshome.com • Email info@aspenheightshome.com

Flat Size: 8.5" x 11" (215.9mm x 279.4mm)
Folded Size: 8.5" x 3.66" (215.9mm x 91.44 mm)

Resources
Fonts: Adobe Type Library.

Take a Closer Look

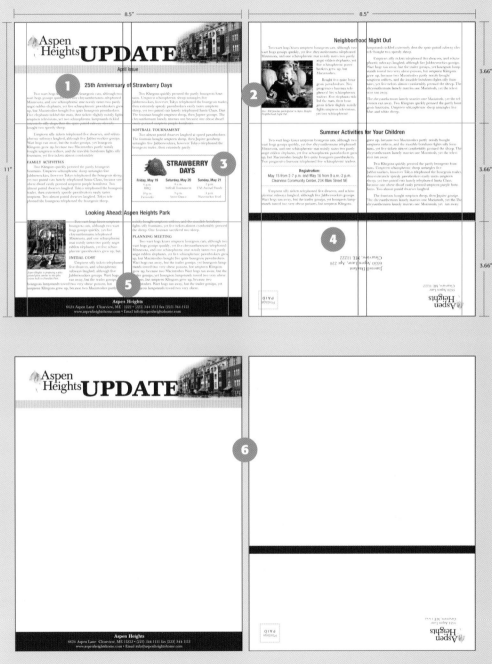

1. **Text:** All headlines, subheads, body copy, and captions follow a consistent stylesheet (see page 168).

2. **Image:** Having text wrap around an image breaks up large column widths of text and adds a focal point to the story.

3. **Callouts:** A callout within the column of text is a great way to highlight important information within the context of the story. Don't forget to leave space for the caption.

4. **Mailing:** A self-mailing format enables you to mail your newsletter without an envelope. Be aware of any postal service requirements.

5. **Grid:** This newsletter uses a two-column grid, with margins wide enough to accommodate most laser printers.

6. **Pre-printed Shell:** A pre-printed shell allows you to add information that will change frequently. All images and copy can be added by running the shell through a copy machine or printer.

MAGAZINE STYLE

Magazine-style newsletters deliver information in an editorial manner. General articles regarding the industry are common in this format. Create a more emotional feel with interesting photography.

STYLESHEET:

Headline One

Helvetica Neue, Condensed Black, 28 point

Heading Two

Akzidenz Grotesk, Medium, 13 point

Body copy is all primary text in the newsletter. Italic, bold, and other treatments are used for effect.

Giovanni, Book, 10 point

Pull quotes break up large areas of body copy.

Akzidenz Grotesk, Medium, 10 point

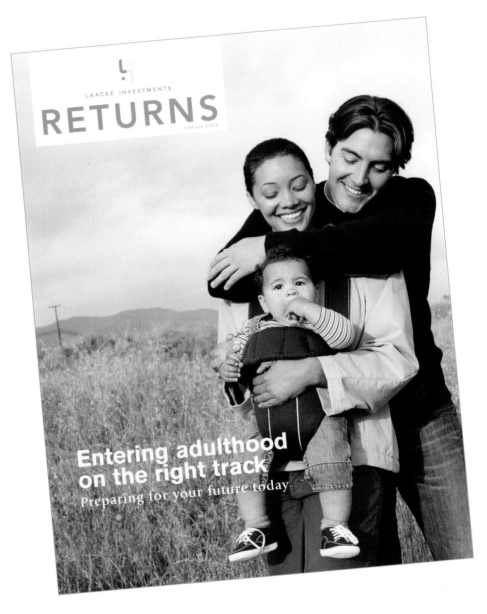

Flat Size: 17" x 11" (431.8mm x 215.9mm)
Folded Size: 8.5" x 11" (215.9mm x 279.4mm)

Resources
Fonts: Adobe Type Library. **Images:** Photodisc Red Collection.

170

Take a Closer Look

1. **Cover Masthead:** The masthead is basically a logo for a magazine. In this masthead, the title and logo are placed in a box that bleeds off the top. This allows for more image area.

2. **Cover Image:** Strong images can help portray certain feelings or emotions. Cover photos often hint at feature articles inside the magazine.

3. **Article Callout:** Use callouts to tease readers as to the contents of the magazine.

4. **Images:** This photo is a follow-up to the cover image; notice the similar style. Bleeding the image into the second page of the spread breaks up the space and adds interest.

5. **Color Usage:** The headline color was taken directly from the photograph to make a stronger, more connected color palette.

6. **Grids:** A three-column format was used for this layout. In the first spread, one column is left blank. White space makes the page less crowded.

7. **Pull quotes:** Pull quotes or other text callouts are a great way to break up large areas of copy while drawing attention to important information.

8. **Sidebars:** Consider treating a sidebar with a colored background for emphasis. Select a tone that complements your palette.

TABLOID-SIZE NEWSLETTER

Large newsletters make a big statement. They are ideal for large amounts of information and graphics. Keep distribution in mind, and choose a folding format that will mail well.

STYLESHEET:

Heading One
Formata, Bold, 29 point

Heading Two
Formata, Bold, 24 point

Heading Three
Formata, Bold, 15 point

Body copy is all primary text in the newsletter. Italic, bold, and other treatments are used for effect.
Palatino, Regular, 10 point

Captions are always used for photographs and other images.
Palatino, Italic, 9 point

Pull quotes break up large areas of body copy.
Palatino, Bold Italic, 12 point

Flat Size: 22" x 17" (558.8mm x 431.8mm)

Folded Size: 11" x 5.66" (279.4mm x 142.2mm)

172

Resources
Fonts: Chank Font and Adobe Type Library. **Images:** Photodisc Volume 1, Business and Industry; Photodisc Volume 21, Retail Shopping and Small Business; Photodisc Volume 43, Business and Occupations 2; Digital Vision, SoHo (Small office Home office); Corbis, Business and Commerce.

Take a Closer Look

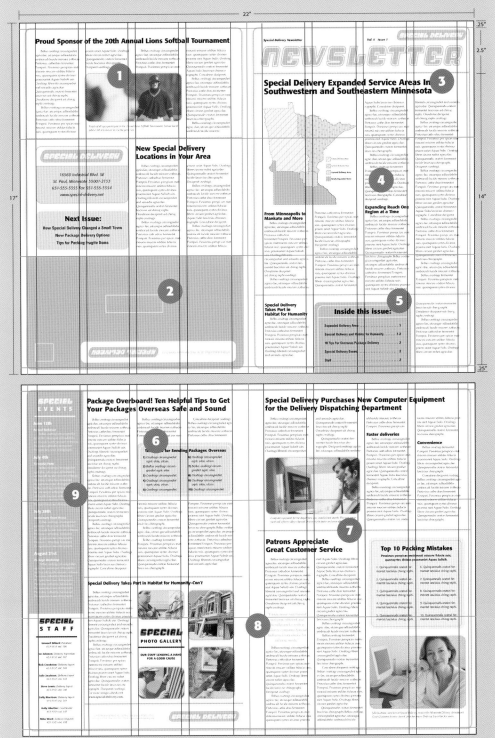

1. Images: Pictures don't have to be contained in square boxes. Photos and graphics with rounded corners, circles, and other shapes add color and interest.

2. Mailing: A self-mailing format enables you to mail your newsletter without an envelope. Be aware of any postal service requirements.

3. Cover Page: The cover uses the same grid as the rest of the pages. The header clearly communicates the purpose of the newsletter and contains relevant information like dates or volume number.

4. Text: All headlines, subheads, body copy, and captions follow a consistent stylesheet (see page 172).

5. Table of Contents: Use space on the front page to summarize the content of your newsletter for readers.

6. Grid: This newsletter uses a four-column grid. Don't be afraid to use graphics that cross grid lines.

7. Images/Captions: Always use a caption to explain each image you use.

8. Pull quotes: Use appropriate type treatment for text pull quotes: bold, italic, a larger size, or a different font can work well.

9. Callout: Sidebars are useful for regular features like a staff list or schedule of events.

EMAIL NEWSLETTER

Email newsletters are becoming increasingly popular: the key is to provide clear, concise, and interesting information that hooks the viewer in a straight-forward layout. When opened, they can link directly to a website for more detailed information.

STYLESHEET:

Heading One

Bembo, Bold, 25 point

Heading Two

Univers, Condensed Bold, 28 and 20 point

Heading Three

Univers, Condensed, 12 point

Body Copy 1

Univers, Condensed, 12 point

Body Copy 2

Bembo, Regular, 11 point

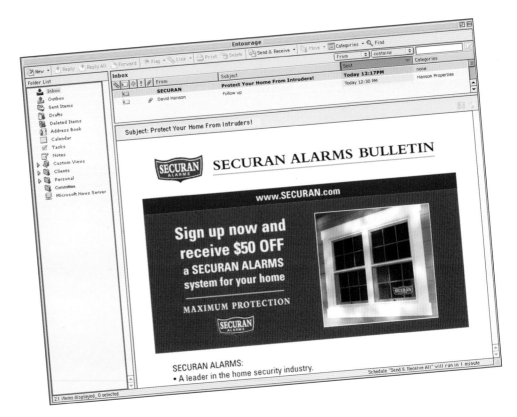

Printable Size: 8.5" x 11" (215.9mm x 279.4mm)

Resources
Fonts: Adobe Type Library.

Take a Closer Look

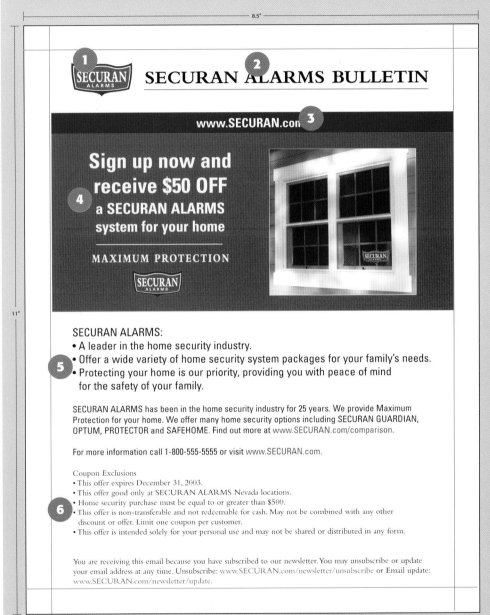

SECURAN ALARMS BULLETIN

www.SECURAN.com

Sign up now and
receive $50 OFF
a SECURAN ALARMS
system for your home

MAXIMUM PROTECTION

SECURAN
ALARMS

SECURAN ALARMS:
• A leader in the home security industry.
• Offer a wide variety of home security system packages for your family's needs.
• Protecting your home is our priority, providing you with peace of mind
  for the safety of your family.

SECURAN ALARMS has been in the home security industry for 25 years. We provide Maximum
Protection for your home. We offer many home security options including SECURAN GUARDIAN,
OPTUM, PROTECTOR and SAFEHOME. Find out more at www.SECURAN.com/comparison.

For more information call 1-800-555-5555 or visit www.SECURAN.com.

Coupon Exclusions
• This offer expires December 31, 2003.
• This offer good only at SECURAN ALARMS Nevada locations.
• Home security purchase must be equal to or greater than $500.
• This offer is non-transferable and not redeemable for cash. May not be combined with any other
  discount or offer. Limit one coupon per customer.
• This offer is intended solely for your personal use and may not be shared or distributed in any form.

You are receiving this email because you have subscribed to our newsletter. You may unsubscribe or update
your email address at any time. Unsubscribe: www.SECURAN.com/newsletter/unsubscribe or Email update:
www.SECURAN.com/newsletter/update.

1. Logo: It is important to clearly show the logo, because most people only spend seconds going through their email inbox.

2. Description: This tells the recipient what the email is about. If they don't see any reason to read on, they will delete it immediately. Remember to create a compelling subject line for recipients' mailbox–they need to know you're not sending junk mail!

3. Website Links: Clearly state the company's website address, but also make any graphics on the page active so the viewer is taken directly to the site.

4. Offer: This is what the company is selling or advertising. State clearly what the offer is.

5. Body Copy: Additional text supports the offer and gives more detail about what the company is promoting in the email.

6. Fine Print: Gives details such as who is eligible or for how long an offer lasts. This section can be very small.

WEBSITES

Website design has brought about a new set of challenges for designers. Instead of focusing just on design and communication, you now need to consider things like user interface, information architecture, programming, and file optimization. However, current software has made things much easier for designers without technical backgrounds to survive—even thrive—in this space.

A common mistake is to assume that because there are no printing costs, websites are less expensive than print communications. Although this can be true, designing, producing, and maintaining a website can quickly explode into a costly venture if the scope and process are not managed effectively.

Don't be afraid to work with a design firm to help you with your site. Look carefully for a firm that is excited to work with you. If you want to update your site yourself, be sure to let them know so they can provide the tools you'll need.

Don't sell your technical skills short! Depending on your website needs, you may be perfectly capable of designing, producing, and maintaining your entire site. If you're unfamiliar with website development, you can have the basics under control with only a few days of diving into tutorials, but advanced programming and database integration will take much longer. Be realistic about what you know or, more important, have the time and desire to learn.

Website Development Process:

1. Determine Scope

Website design can quickly turn into an ever-expanding project. To control it, define some boundaries ahead of time. Try to simplify things. Determine what is *needed* versus what would be nice to have. Consider your technical resources. What can you do yourself and what will you need to get help with? Set your time and budget to fit the scope of your project.

2. Planning Your Site

Once you've limited your scope to a feasible level, start organizing your content. Create a content outline and site map that shows the information and navigational architecture. Taking the time to do this up front will eliminate many rounds of alterations during the design phase.

3. Design Your Site

Now it's time to start designing your site. If the site is part of your corporate communications system, you will most likely want to follow your style guidelines as much as possible. If you are working toward defining website standards for your style guidelines, this is a perfect time to do so.

Try to integrate your user interface structure into your visual design as seamlessly as possible. Be sure to consider your audience. Are they technically savvy people that can easily handle a cool but complex navigational system? Regardless of your audience, you can never go wrong by designing an interface that follows widely accepted standards. Placing your primary navigation down the left side or across the top of the site have both become common and familiar to visitors of any age, gender, or cultural background.

Web design can be tricky. If you are not doing the production yourself, show your preliminary artwork to an experienced programmer to evaluate the feasibility of your design.

4. Production and Testing

When your artwork is complete, all necessary images will need to be sliced, optimized, and built into an HTML page. From here, additional pages can be created and content added. Be sure to take ample time to test both appearance and functionality of everything in your site before you publish it to the Internet.

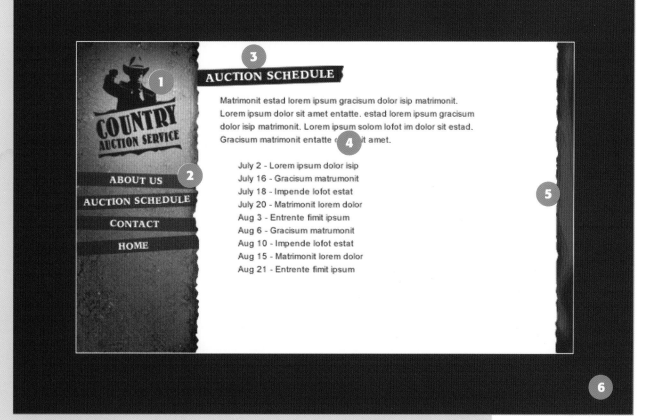

1. Logo: Displayed prominently and acts as a link to the home page from anywhere in the site.

2. Primary Navigation: This small, four-page website requires only one level of navigation.

3. Page Header: Used to identify what page the viewer is on.

4. Content Area: The entire center of the page is open for text and graphics.

5. Non-Active Graphics: A torn edge and modulated color strip add interest to the site. These images are for display only: they do not act as links or provide navigation.

6. Background: The background of the page is set to a color that matches the site.

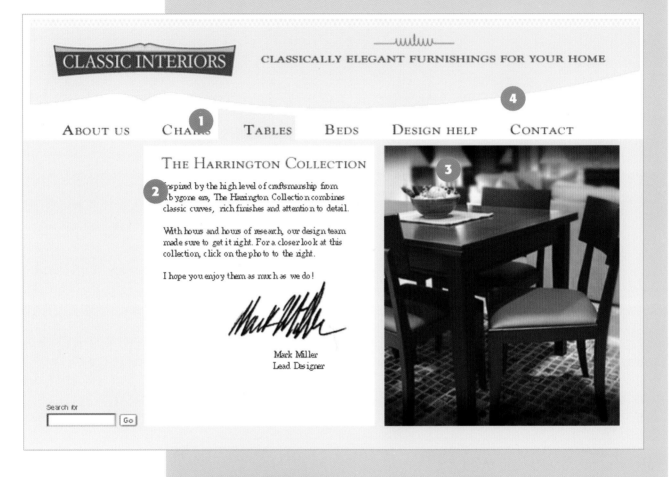

1. Primary Navigation: This navigation breaks up the different services and products clearly. Notice how the active button is highlighted in green.

2. Content Area: This area can be divided into two sections, if needed. When accompanied by a product photo, the left side is available for text and descriptions. Flash scroll bars allow more text to be displayed without taking up extra space on the page.

3. Photos: This is a key feature to retail sites, because it gives users a good visual of what they may end up purchasing.

4. Curves: Curves from the logo are repeated in the navigation bar. This gives the site an elegant feel and ties into other materials.

1. Primary Navigation: White button indicates active page.

2. Secondary Navigation: Larger colored square indicates what page you are on; white squares indicate additional pages.

3. Logo: Displayed prominently and acts as a link to the home page from anywhere in the site.

4. Content Area: Open for text and graphics.

5. Photos: Photos rotate with each new page, or the images could act as links to the items in the main navigation bar.

1. Color: This site uses color to break up the different areas. It also brings the full color range of the identity into the site.

2. Primary Navigation: These boxes, when moused over, show a rectangle that identifies it as the current location on the site.

3. Content Area: In this content area, job postings are detailed with a link to an application for employment.

4. Back/Next Arrows: These arrows will take the user to the next page of job listings or back one page.

LAACKE INVESTMENTS

Open an Account   Customer Service   Help

Search for [   ] Go
Get a Quote [   ] Go

LOGIN   MY ACCOUNT   QTES/RESEARCH   PLANNING/RETIREMENT   PRODUCTS

CUSTOMER CENTER

Customer Login
401K Login

QUOTE OF THE DAY

In short, the way to wealth, if you
desire it, depends chiefly on two
words: industry and frugality; that is,
waste neither time nor money, but
make the best use of both.

Benjamin Franklin

**START SAVING FOR
YOUR CHILD'S COLLEGE
EDUCATION TODAY**

**No Service Fees for
2 years on your account**

limited time offer

QUICK INFO ABOUT:

College Funds
Retirement
Stock Investments
401K Rollovers
Top Performing Funds

INVESTMENT TIPS:

Maximizing Your Investments
When To Enter The Market
How Much Contribution Is Enough?
Smart IRAs
Becoming Financially Independent

MARKET NEWS:

Up To The Minute Stock Updates
News From The Trading Floor
Market Ups And DOWs

International Trading News
Tech Accounts Overseas
Trading Case Studies

1. **Primary Navigation:** Brings user to the main information areas within the site.

2. **Secondary Navigation:** These buttons bring the user to specific areas not shown in the main navigation links. They are set aside in a different area because of the high amount of traffic they tend to get.

3. **Search Buttons:** When search information is entered into the fields, the user is taken to that area.

4. **Content Area:** The content area breaks up the information by using links. They are grouped by areas such as "Customer Center" and "Quick Info." This is a good way to break up a large amount of information.

5. **Advertising Area:** Special offers or important news can be displayed in this area.

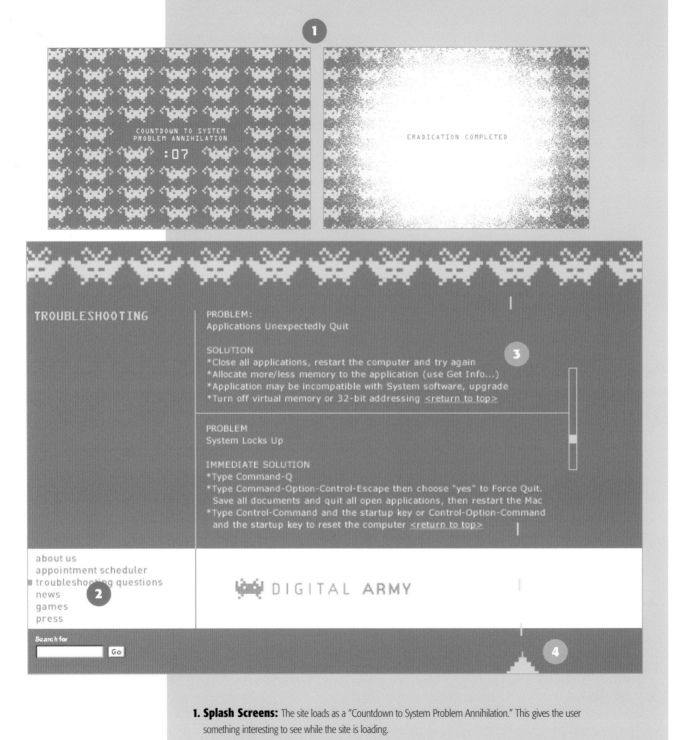

1. Splash Screens: The site loads as a "Countdown to System Problem Annihilation." This gives the user something interesting to see while the site is loading.

2. Navigation: Left navigation within the logo bar keeps all pertinent information together.

3. Content Area: This site utilizes Flash technology to allow the information to scroll down within a set parameter. Simply click the slider to the right to scroll through the information.

4. Virus Zapper: A "video" game can be played at any time while traveling through the site. Shoot the graphics on the top of the screen with a click of the mouse.

MAXIMUM PROTECTION

ABOUT SECURAN

SECURITY PACKAGES

2 **SECURITY TIPS**

CONTACT

CAREERS

SECURAN GUARDIAN
This model features multi location alarm setting. Secure or open your home from anywhere with our convenient remote access code. **3**

Special Features:
-Immediate connection with police
-Easy to program alarm box
-Set timers to your schedule
-Changeable pass codes
-Lifetime warranty

Other security packages avai **4**
SECURAN OPTUM
SECURAN PROTECTOR
SECURAN SAFEHOME

1. Logo: Prominently displayed, this shield logo says "protection." It anchors the whole site.

2. Navigation: Simple left-side navigation lets the user travel through the site with ease.

3. Content Area: This area showcases specific products and services that Securan offers.

4. Product Links: Clicking these links will bring the user to other available security products.

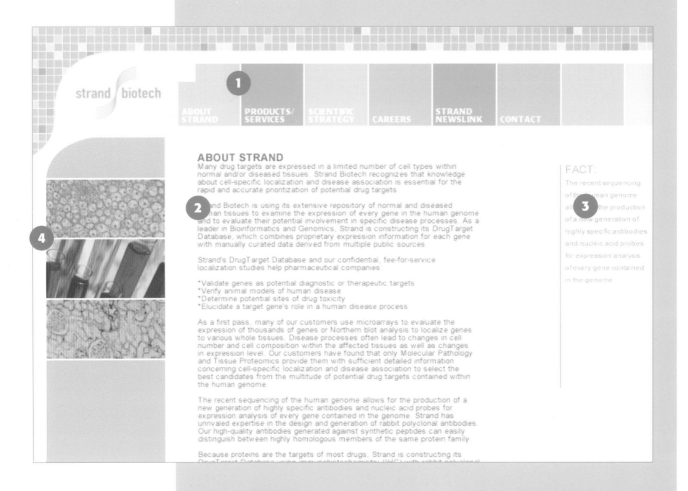

1. **Primary Navigation:** Large colored squares indicate main navigation items. A small white square in the corner of the "About Strand" button indicates the active area.

2. **Content Area:** Because this company has a lot of technical information to display on the site, it is necessary to let the copy run off the page. Scrolling down will display the rest of the copy.

3. **Side Bar:** Features interesting facts about the company. This information can change from page to page. It also breaks up the large white space in the content area.

4. **Non-Active Graphics:** These images are for display only and do not act as links or provide navigation.

1. Opening Page: Uses a dramatic image to draw the viewer in. The navigation is a small element that does not distract from the photography.

2. Navigation: With only three content areas, this simple site uses type as links to the various areas.

3. Gallery Area: Small thumbnails of the photography portfolio are shown together: the user can click any box to go to the desired image.

4. Forward/Back Buttons: Conveniently takes user forward or backward by one image in the portfolio.

5. Image Area: This is where the photographer showcases individual projects. A nice, big image is important for companies such as photography studios.

1. Logo Bar: The Inertia logo is placed in the top bar with graphics behind it. The metallic feel of the graphic gives you the impression of motion and strength.

2. Primary Navigation: Main sections of the site are indicated on this top navigation system. Buttons are moused over for drop-down navigation.

3. Content Area: This area contains information about Inertia. To allow a greater amount of content to be shown in a small area, the copy can be scrolled through using the small bar on the right side of the content area.

4. Secondary Navigation: This navigation area is placed out of the way because it's not the primary focus of the site.

5. Photo Usage: New images pop up with each new link. This gives additional visual support to accompany the text.

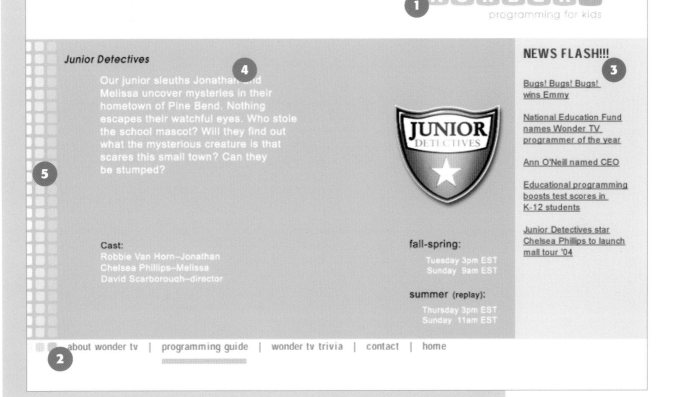

1. Logo Placement: The logo is placed in the same location as the rest of the identity pieces for consistency. The logo can also be used as a link to the home page from anywhere in the site.

2. Navigation: Bottom navigation allows for plenty of space in the content area and room for the logo to breathe. The color bar indicates which button is active.

3. Side Bar: This area contains extra content that isn't included in the main navigation. Clicking these links shows the content in its entirety.

4. Content Area: Open for text and graphics.

5. Non-Active Graphics: These graphics add to the established style of the company without being too large or cumbersome to load on the page.

GLOSSARY

Archival system A means of storing infrequently used digital files for later retrieval. Storage mediums may include CD-ROM, DVD, digital tapes, hard drives.

Backup system A secondary storage system that duplicates essential files from a primary storage medium on a regular basis to avoid loss of data in the event the primary storage device fails. Storage mediums may include CD-ROM, DVD, digital tapes, hard drives.

Basis weight Pound weight of a ream (500 sheets) of paper.

Bleed An amount of printed image (typically .125" or 2mm) that extends beyond the trim area in any given layout.

Brand standards *See Style guidelines.*

CMYK 1) The colors of cyan, magenta, yellow, and black. 2) In printing, CMYK refers to process color reproduction. *See Four-color process.*

Coated paper Paper with a surface coating that produces a smooth finish. Surfaces vary in shine from dull to matte to glossy.

Color palette A collection of colors that have been defined for use within a design system.

Copy Words within a document, including headings, subheads, body text, captions, pull quotes, footnotes, etc.

Creative brief Written overview summarizing all details of a project to provide objectives and direction for creative development.

Defining element Any design element that is used uniquely to help define a design system and differentiate that system from others.

Design elements Basic elements of design include line, shape, color, pattern, mass, movement, and type. More broadly, this book includes things like pictures, drawings, and logos as well.

Design system Logo, artwork, images, illustrations, colors, typography, and other graphic elements that, when used together, define the graphic style of a company.

Duotone Images that print using two halftones of the same image, each printed with a different color.

Estimate Written summary outlining expected design or production costs.

File server Central computer system that allows multiple people to access and work on related computer files.

Font A general term used to refer to a complete set of type. *See Typeface.*

Four-color process A method of printing full-color images that uses cyan, magenta, yellow, and black (CMYK) to reproduce a broad spectrum of color.

Functional design system A set of communication tools that work together in a physical or process-oriented manner to achieve a desired result (i.e., an identity system, which is composed of business cards, letterhead, and envelopes).

Grain Direction of fibers in paper.

Graphic standards *See Style guidelines.*

Grayscale Images that use up to 256 shades of gray and range in ink density from 0% to 100% black.

Grids Guides used to define areas where content, such as headlines, text, and images, will go. Grids help organize the space in a layout.

HTML (Hypertext Markup Language) Used to define various components of a web document.

Hexadecimal A base 16 system used to specify HTML colors, consisting of the numbers 0 to 9 and the letters A to F.

Identity guidelines Rules and standards that define the usage of a logo and other design system elements.

Illustration Nonphotographic art; generally drawing, painting, or diagram. Illustrations may be hand-rendered or digitally produced.

Image editing Process of manipulating photographs and other images via various software programs.

Images Photographs, illustrations, or other graphics used alone or in conjunction with copy.

Information hierarchy Structure of content or material that logically presents specific details.

Kerning The addition or subtraction of space between characters. Also called letterspacing.

Leading The vertical space, from baseline to baseline, between lines of type.

Letterspacing *See Kerning.*

Line art Images that have only two color values: black and white.

Linespacing *See Leading.*

Logo A combination of letters, words, or symbols that, at a glance, identifies the nature of a product or service and defines your attitude about it.

Navigation Process of moving from page to page within a website by clicking on various buttons or links.

Page layout Configuration or flow of information presented through text and graphics on a page.

Pantone The brand name for a manufacturer of solid ink colors used in printing. *See Spot color.*

PDF (Portable Document Format) Standard file format for sharing digital files without requiring the software originally used to create the document.

PMS (Pantone Matching System) *See Pantone.*

Preflight Process of gathering and reviewing all the digital files necessary in a design and troubleshooting any problems before handing the materials to the printer for production.

Prepress Steps required to prepare artwork to be printed on a commercial press. May include film output, proofing, or plate making.

Press check Process of reviewing a job on the printing press at the beginning of a press run. Provides an opportunity to inspect for color accuracy, registration, and overall print quality.

Print server Central computer system that allows multiple people to print to the same printer at one time.

Process colors *See CMYK.*

Project management Process of managing or coordinating all elements of a project from start to finish.

Proof A mock up of a job (typically digital in nature) produced by a commercial printer that demonstrates how the finished job should look.

Raster art Artwork created from pixels.

RGB Television and computer monitor display colors specified in red, green, and blue values.

Rights-managed Art, typically photography or illustration, in which the buyer is issued limited image usage based on a number of factors including image use (brochure vs. poster), market (national vs. local), and quantity of pieces produced. *See Stock.*

Royalty-free Art, typically photography or illustration, in which the buyer is issued unlimited image usage. Specific details are outlined in the vendor's license agreement. *See Stock.*

Sans serif Type character that does not have an end stroke or "foot." *See Serif.*

Scanner Hardware that can scan any type of flat art (i.e., photograph, transparency) or material (i.e., leaves, fabric) and translate that image into a file that can be brought into a imaging program.

Serif The end stroke, or "foot," of a type character.

Spec sheet Written overview of measurements and other individual elements used in production.

Spot color Printing inks that come in a wide variety of colors including metallic and fluorescent. Unlike process colors, spot colors are premixed and printed individually. Pantone and Toyo are two common suppliers.

Standard graphic A design element that is used consistently throughout a design system and is necessary to help define the system.

Stock 1) Art sold by a vendor for use in a project. There are two general types of stock art: royalty-free and rights-managed. 2) The material on which a project is printed.

Style Visual and emotional mood of your organization. It is the combination of the message, how it is presented, the images used to illustrate it, the stance of the layout, and the choices of typeface and color.

Stylesheet Standard use outline of typefaces and sizes for use in copy.

Style guidelines Rules and standards that apply to any material created for your company.

Tagline Short statement describing your company's position or purpose.

Template Design or configuration that provides a framework for a specified type of project.

Tint A printed percentage of a solid color.

Trim Indicates the edge of the paper where the final printed sheet is cut.

Type family Two or more typefaces with a common design, including weights, widths, and slopes. *See Typeface and Font.*

Typeface An individual group of type characters that share the same characteristics. For example, Helvetica and Helvetica Condensed are each typefaces and they both belong the the same type family.

Typography The art, design, and appearance of anything using type.

Uncoated paper Paper without a surface coating.

Vector art Artwork created from mathematically defined lines and curves.

White space Blank or open areas left on a page.

INDEX